THE CENTURY HANDBOOK
OF WRITING

THE
CENTURY HANDBOOK SERIES

THE CENTURY HANDBOOK OF WRITING.
   By Garland Greever and Easley S. Jones.

THE CENTURY VOCABULARY BUILDER.
   By Garland Greever and Joseph M. Bachelor.

THE CENTURY DESK BOOK OF GOOD ENGLISH.
   By Garland Greever and Joseph M. Bachelor.

A BUSINESS MAN'S DESK BOOK.
   By Garland Greever and Joseph M. Bachelor.

THE FACTS AND BACKGROUNDS OF LITERATURE, English and
   American. By George F. Reynolds, University of
   Colorado, and Garland Greever.

PARLIAMENTARY PRACTICE.
   By General Henry M. Robert.

Other Volumes To Be Arranged

THE CENTURY HANDBOOK OF WRITING

BY

GARLAND GREEVER

AND

EASLEY S. JONES

Revised Edition

NEW YORK
THE CENTURY CO.
1925

Copyright, 1918, 1922, by
THE CENTURY CO.

Printed in U. S. A.

PREFACE

This handbook treats essential matters of grammar, diction, spelling, mechanics; and develops with thoroughness the principles of sentence structure. Larger units of composition it leaves to the texts in formal rhetoric.

The book is built on a decimal plan, the material being simplified and reduced to one hundred articles. Headings of these articles are summarized on two opposite pages by a chart. Here the student can see at a glance the resources of the volume, and the instructor can find immediately the number he wishes to write in the margin of a theme. The chart and the decimal scheme together make the rules accessible for instant reference.

By a device equally efficient, the book throws upon the student the responsibility of teaching himself. Each article begins with a concise rule, which is illustrated by examples; then follows a short "parallel exercise" which the instructor may assign by adding an x to the number he writes in the margin of a theme. While correcting this exercise, the student will give attention to the rule, and will acquire theory and practice at the same time. Moreover, every group of ten articles is followed by mixed exercises; these may be used for review, or imposed in the margin of a theme as a penalty for flagrant or repeated error. Thus friendly counsel is backed by discipline, and the instructor has the means of compelling the student to make rapid progress toward good English.

Although a handbook of this nature is in some ways arbitrary, the arbitrariness is always in the interest of simplicity. The book does have simplicity, permits instant reference, and provides an adequate drill which may be assigned at the stroke of a pen.

TABLE OF CONTENTS

SENTENCE STRUCTURE

COMPLETENESS OF THOUGHT
1. Fragments wrongly used as sentences
2. Incomplete constructions
3. Necessary words omitted
4. Comparisons not logically completed
5. Cause and reason
6. *Is when* and *is where* clauses
7. Undeveloped thought
8. Transitions
9. EXERCISE
   A. Incomplete sentences
   B. Incomplete constructions
   C. Incomplete logic
   D. Undeveloped thought and transitions

UNITY OF THOUGHT
10. Independent ideas in one sentence
11. Excessive detail
12. Stringy sentences to be broken up
13. Choppy sentences to be combined
14. Excessive coördination
15. Faulty subordination of the main thought
16. Subordination thwarted by *and*
17. The *and which* construction
18. The comma splice
19. EXERCISE
    A. The comma splice
    B. One thought in a sentence
    C. Excessive coördination
    D. Excessive predication
    E. Upside-down subordination

CONTENTS

CLEARNESS OF THOUGHT

REFERENCE
20. Divided reference
21. Weak reference
22. Broad reference
23. Dangling participle or gerund

COHERENCE
24. General incoherence
25. Logical sequence
26. Squinting modifier
27. Misplaced word
28. Split construction
29. EXERCISE
    A. Reference of pronouns
    B. Dangling modifiers
    C. Coherence

PARALLEL STRUCTURE
30. Parallel structure for parallel thoughts
31. Correlatives

CONSISTENCY
32. Shift in subject or voice
33. Shift in number, person, or tense
34. Mixed constructions
35. Mixed imagery

USE OF CONNECTIVES
36. The exact connective
37. Repetition of connective with gain in clearness
38. Repetition of connective with loss in clearness

39. EXERCISE
    A. Parallel structure
    B. Shift in subject or voice
    C. Shift in number, person, or tense
    D. The exact connective
    E. Subordinating connectives
    F. Repetition of connectives

CONTENTS

EMPHASIS

40. Emphasis by position
41. Emphasis by separation
42. Emphasis by subordination
43. The periodic sentence
44. Order of climax
45. The balanced sentence
46. Weak effect of the passive voice
47. Repetition effective: a Words; b Structure
48. Repetition offensive: a Words; b Structure
49. EXERCISE
    A. Lack of emphasis in general
    B. Loose structure
    C. Repetition

GRAMMAR

50. Case: a Nominative, especially after *than* or *as;* b Nominative *who* and *whoever;* c Predicate nominative; d Objective; e Objective with infinitive; f Possessive; g Possessive with gerund; h Possession by inanimate objects; i Agreement of pronouns
51. Number: a *Each, every one*, etc.; b *Those kind*, etc.; c Collective nouns; d *Don't*
52. Agreement—not to be thwarted by: a Intervening nouns; b *Together with* phrases; c *Or* or *nor* after subject; d *And* in the subject; e A predicate noun; f An introductory *there*
53. *Shall* and *will*
54. Principal parts. List
55. Tense, mode, auxiliaries: a Tense in dependent clauses or infinitives; b The past perfect; c Present tense for a general statement; d Mode; e Auxiliaries
56. Adjective and adverb: a Adjective misused for adverb; b Ambiguous cases; c After verbs pertaining to the senses
57. A word in a double capacity
58. List of the terms of grammar

CONTENTS

59. EXERCISE
    - A. Case of pronouns
    - B. Agreement
    - C. *Shall* and *will*
    - D. *Lie, lay; sit, set; rise, raise*
    - E. Principal parts of verbs
    - F. General

DICTION

60. Wordiness
61. Triteness
62. The exact word
63. Concreteness
64. Sound
65. Subtle violations of good use: a Faulty idiom; b Colloquialism
66. Gross violations of good use: a Barbarisms; b Improprieties; c Slang
67. Words often confused in meaning. List
68. Glossary of faulty diction
69. EXERCISE
    - A. Wordiness
    - B. The exact word
    - C. Words sometimes confused in meaning
    - D. Colloquialisms, slang, faulty idioms

SPELLING

70. Recording errors
71. Pronouncing accurately
72. Logical kinship in words
73. Superficial resemblances. List
74. Words in *ei* and *ie*
75. Doubling a final consonant
76. Dropping final *e*
77. Plurals: a Plurals in *s* or *es;* b Nouns ending in *y;* c Compound nouns; d Letters, figures, and signs; e Old plurals; f Foreign plurals
78. Compounds: a Compound adjectives; b Compound nouns; c Numbers; d Words written solid; e General principle
79. SPELLING LIST (500 words, 200 in bold-face type)

CONTENTS

MISCELLANEOUS

80. Manuscript: a Titles; b Spacing; c Handwriting
81. Capitals: a To begin a sentence or a quotation; b Proper names; c Proper adjectives; d In titles of books or themes; e Miscellaneous uses
82. Italics: a Titles of books; b Foreign words; c Names of ships; d Words taken out of context; e For emphasis
83. Abbreviations: a In ordinary writing; b In business writing
84. Numbers: a Dates and street numbers; b Long figures; c Sums of money, etc.
85. Syllabication: a Position of hyphen; b Division between syllables; c Monosyllabic words not divided; d One consonant between syllables; e Two consonants between syllables; f Prefixes and suffixes; g Short words.
86. Outlines: a Topic Outline; b Sentence Outline; c Paragraph Outline; d Indention; e Parallel form; f Faulty coördination; g Too detailed subordination
87. Letters: a Heading; b Inside address and greeting; c Body, Language; d Close; e Outside address; f Miscellaneous directions; g Model business letter; h Formal notes
88. Paragraphs: a Indention; b Length; c Dialogue
89. EXERCISE
    Capitals, numbers, abbreviations, etc.

PUNCTUATION

90. The Period: a After sentences; b But not after fragments of sentences; c After abbreviations
91. The Comma: a Between clauses joined by *but, for, and;* b But NOT to splice clauses not joined by a conjunction; c After a subordinate clause preceding a main clause; d To set off non-restrictive clauses and phrases; e To set off parenthetical elements; f Between adjectives; g Between words in a series; h Before a quotation; i To compel a pause for clearness; j Superfluous uses
92. The Semicolon: a Between coördinate clauses not joined by a conjunction; b Between long coördinate clauses; c Before a formal conjunctive adverb; d But not before a quotation

CONTENTS

93. The Colon: a To introduce a formal series or quotation; b Before concrete illustrations of a previous general statement
94. The Dash: a To enclose a parenthetical statement; b To mark a breaking-off in thought; c Before a summarizing statement; d But not to be used in place of a period; e Not to be confused with the hyphen
95. Parenthesis Marks: a Uses; b With other marks; c Confirmatory symbols; d Not used to cancel words; e Brackets
96. Quotation Marks: a With quotations; b With paragraphs; c In dialogue; d With slang, etc.; e With words set apart; f Quotation within a quotation; g Together with other marks; h Quotation interrupted by *he said;* i Omission from a quotation; j Unnecessary in the title of a theme, or as a label for humor or irony
97. The Apostrophe: a In contractions; b To form the possessive; c To form the possessive of nouns ending in *s;* d Not used with personal possessive pronouns; e To form the plural of certain signs and letters
98. The Question Mark: a After a direct question; b Not followed by a comma within a sentence; c In parentheses to express uncertainty; d Not used to label irony; e The Exclamation Point
99. EXERCISE IN PUNCTUATION
100. GENERAL EXERCISE

TO THE STUDENT

When a number is written in the margin of your theme, you are to turn to the article which corresponds to the number. Read the rule (printed in bold-face type), and study the examples. When an *r* follows the number on your theme, you are, in addition, to copy the rule. When an *x* follows the number, you are, besides acquainting yourself with the rule, to write the exercise of five sentences, to correct your own faulty sentence, and to hand in the six on theme paper. If the number ends in 9 (9, 19, 29, etc.), you will find, not a rule, but a long exercise which you are to write and hand in on theme paper. In the absence of special instructions from your teacher, you are invariably to proceed as this paragraph requires.

Try to grasp the principle which underlies the rule. In many places in this book the reason for the existence of the rule is clearly stated. Thus under 30, the reason for the rule on parallel structure is explained in a prologue. In other instances, as in the rule on divided reference (20), the reason becomes clear the moment you read the examples. In certain other instances the rule may appear arbitrary and without a basis in reason. But there is a basis in reason, as you will observe in the following illustration.

Suppose you write, "He is twenty one years old." The instructor asks you to put a hyphen in *twenty-one,* and refers you to 78. You cannot see why a hyphen is necessary, since the meaning is clear without it. But tomorrow you may write, "I will send you twenty five dollar bills." The reader cannot tell whether you mean twenty five-dollar bills or twenty-five dollar bills. In the first sentence the use of the hyphen in *twenty-one* did not make much difference. In the second sentence the hyphen makes seventy-five dollars' worth of difference. Thus the instructor, in asking you to write, "He is twenty-one years old," is helping you to form a habit that will save you from serious error in other sentences. Whenever you cannot understand the reason for a rule, ask yourself whether the usage of many clear-thinking men for long years past may not be protecting you from difficulties which you do not foresee. Instructors and writers of text books (impressive as is the evidence to the contrary) are human, and do not invent rules to puzzle you. They do not, in fact, invent rules at all, but only make convenient applications of principles which generations of writers have found to be wisest and best.

THE CENTURY HANDBOOK
OF WRITING

SENTENCE STRUCTURE
COMPLETENESS OF THOUGHT

The first thing to make certain is that the thought of a sentence is complete. A fragment which has no meaning when read alone, or a sentence from which is omitted a necessary word, phrase, or idea, violates an elementary principle of writing.

Fragments Wrongly Used as Sentences

1. Do not write a subordinate part of a sentence as if it were a complete sentence.

Wrong: He stopped short. Hearing some one approach.
Right: He stopped short, hearing some one approach. [Or] Hearing some one approach, he stopped short.
Wrong: The winters are cold. Although the summers are pleasant.
Right: Although the summers are pleasant, the winters are cold.
Wrong: The hunter tried to move the stone. Which he found very heavy.
Right: The hunter tried to move the stone, which he found very heavy. [Or] The hunter tried to move the stone. He found it very heavy.

Note.—A sentence must in itself express a complete thought. Phrases or subordinate clauses, if used alone, carry only an incomplete meaning. They must therefore be attached to a sentence, or restated in independent form. Elliptical expressions used in conversation may be regarded as exceptions: Where? At what time? Ten o'clock. By no means. Certainly. Go.

COMPLETENESS OF THOUGHT

Exercise:

1. No one could close the door. The lock having been broken.
2. Joseph was the oldest son of Jacob and Rachel. Also his father's favorite son.
3. Glendower was obliged to flee into the hills to save his life. Often living for days on such food as nature provided, and sleeping in caves.
4. Two conditions stimulated emigration to America. The pressure of the population in Europe. And opportunity to secure high wages and virtually free land in America.
5. I have had little success with my camera. Which I am just learning to use. A photographer has volunteered to teach me how to make the exposures properly. So that I hope for better results soon.

Incomplete Constructions

2. Do not leave uncompleted a construction which you have begun.

Wrong: You remember that in his speech in which he said he would oppose the bill.

Right: You remember that in his speech he said he would oppose the bill. [Or] You remember the speech in which he said he would oppose the bill.

Wrong: He was a young man who, coming from the country, with ignorance of city ways, but with plenty of determination to succeed.

Right: He was a young man who, coming from the country, was ignorant of city ways, but had plenty of determination to succeed.

Wrong: From the window of the train I perceived one of those unsightly structures.

Right: From the window of the train I perceived one of those unsightly structures which are always to be seen near a station.

COMPLETENESS OF THOUGHT

Exercise:

1. As far as his improving the service, he is one of those political postmasters.
2. Men who have actually drilled and fought, the glory of military life is no inducement to them.
3. The salad dressing, because it seemed to taste a little strange, everybody hesitated to eat it.
4. By flooding the market with the first series of bonds made it hard to dispose of the later bonds.
5. The actors having no dressing rooms they had to dress wherever they could find a place was available.

Necessary Words Omitted

3. Do not omit a word or a phrase which is necessary to an immediate understanding of a sentence.

Ambiguous: I consulted the secretary and president. [Did the speaker consult one man or two?]

Right: I consulted the secretary and the president. [Or] I consulted the president who is also the secretary.

Ambiguous: Water passes through the cement as well as the bricks.

Right: Water passes through the cement as well as through the bricks.

Wrong: I have had experience in every phase of the automobile.

Right: I have had experience in every phase of automobile driving and repairing.

Wrong: About him were men whom he could not tell whether they were friends or foes.

Right: About him were men regarding whom he could not tell whether they were friends or foes. [Or, better] About him were men who might have been either friends or foes.

Exercise:

1. When four years old, my father brought me a white fox which he had shot.

COMPLETENESS OF THOUGHT

2. Another instance, when a man buys a house he should see that the title is clear.
3. Each door has a number. This way the students have no trouble finding classrooms.
4. The pier extended out a mile into the lake. We had gone there many times and no accidents.
5. Received your letter several days ago. Was very pleased to hear from you. Have a room in such a pretty house. It has six rooms and very well furnished.

Comparisons

4. Comparisons must be completed logically.

Wrong: His speed was equal to a racehorse.
Wrong: Of course my opinion is worth less than a lawyer.
Wrong: The shells which are used in quail hunting are different than in rabbit hunting.

Compare a thing with another thing, an abstraction with another abstraction. Do not carelessly compare a thing with a part or quality of another thing. Always ask yourself: What is compared with what?

Right: His speed was equal to that of a racehorse.
Right: Of course my opinion is worth less than a lawyer's.
Right: The shells used in quail hunting are different from those used in rabbit hunting.

Self-contradictory: Chicago is larger than any city in Illinois.
Right: Chicago is larger than any other city in Illinois.

Impossible: Chicago is the largest of any other city in Illinois.
Right: Chicago is the largest of all the cities in Illinois. [Or] Chicago is the largest city in Illinois.

Note.—After a comparative, the subject of the comparison should be excluded from the class to which it is

COMPLETENESS OF THOUGHT

compared; after a superlative, the subject of the comparison should be included within the class.

Wrong: {taller of all the girls
tallest of any girl

Right: {taller than any other girl [comparative]
tallest of all the girls [superlative]

Exercise:
1. The work of this little typewriter equals the expensive machines.
2. It gives the most light of any other kind of reflector.
3. Horace Greeley's education was of a type different from most men.
4. This airplane is a comfortable machine, and travel in it is easier than a railway coach.
5. Achilles was the bravest of any other of the Greeks. The *Majestic* is larger than all passenger ships on the Atlantic.

Cause and Reason

5. A simple statement of fact may be completed by a *because* clause.

Right: I am late because I was sick.

But a statement containing *the reason is* must be completed by a *that* clause.

Wrong: The reason I am late is because I was sick. [The "reason" is not a "because"; the "reason" is the fact of sickness.]

Right: The reason I am late is that I was sick.

Because, the conjunction, may introduce an adverbial clause only.

Wrong: Because a man wears old clothes is no proof that he is poor. [A *because* clause cannot be the subject of *is*.]

COMPLETENESS OF THOUGHT

Right: The fact that a man wears old clothes is no proof that he is poor. [Or] The wearing of old clothes is not proof that a man is poor.

Note.—*Because of* and *on account of* introduce adverbial phrases only. *Due to* and *caused by* introduce adjectival phrases only.

Wrong: He failed, due to weak eyes. [*Due* is an adjective; it cannot modify a verb.]

Right: His failure was $\begin{Bmatrix} \text{due to} \\ \text{caused by} \end{Bmatrix}$ weak eyes.

Right: He failed $\begin{Bmatrix} \text{because of} \\ \text{on account of} \end{Bmatrix}$ weak eyes.

Exercise:

1. Potatoes contain starch is the reason the doctor says I shouldn't eat them.
2. My reason for studying agriculture is because I intend to be a farmer.
3. The reason he rushed down the stairway was because the fire escape was crowded.
4. Because the roots of his tooth might be ulcerated led him to have the X-ray taken.
5. He strangled, caused by trying to breathe under water.

is when or *is where* Clauses

6. Do not use a *when* or *where* clause as a predicate noun. Do not define a word by saying it is a "when" or a "where". Define a noun by another noun, a verb by another verb, etc.

Wrong: The great event is when the train arrives.
Right: The great event is the arrival of the train.

Wrong: Immigration is where foreigners come into a country.

COMPLETENESS OF THOUGHT

Right: Immigration is the entering of foreigners into a country.
Wrong: A simile is when one object is compared with another.
Right: A simile is a figure of speech in which one object is compared with another.

Note.—A definition of a term is a statement which (1) names the class to which the term belongs, and (2) distinguishes it from other members of the class. Example: A quadrilateral is a plane figure having four sides and four angles. To test a definition ask whether it separates the term defined from all other things. If the definition does not do this, it is incomplete. Define *California* (so as to exclude other states), *window* (so as to exclude *door*), *star* (exclude *moon*), *night, rain, circle, Bible, metal, mile, rectangle*.

Exercise:
1. A submarine is when a boat can operate beneath the surface of the water.
2. Every one knows that the "Single Tax" is where only land is taxed.
3. The definition of astronomy is when one studies the stars and other heavenly bodies.
4. Coöperative buying is where a whole class or community bands together to eliminate the middleman's profits.
5. I feel that one of my mistakes, speaking from the standpoint of money, was when I left the farm.

Undeveloped Thought

7. Do not halfway express an idea. If the idea is important, develop it. If it is not important, omit it.

Incomplete: Haunted houses, in my opinion, is only a superstition.

COMPLETENESS OF THOUGHT

Right: The belief that houses can be haunted is, in my opinion, only a superstition.

Puzzling: McAndrew had inherited money, his suitcase being plastered with labels.

Right: Since McAndrew had inherited money, he had traveled extensively. His suitcase was plastered with the labels of foreign hotels.

Careless: In looking for gasoline troubles, we forgot to see whether the tank was supplied.

Right: In looking for the cause of the trouble, we forgot to see whether the tank was supplied with gasoline.

Note.—In giving information about books, do not confuse the title with the contents or some part of the contents. Be accurate in referring to the time, scene, action, plot, or characters.

Loose thinking: Shakespeare's *Hamlet* occurs in Denmark [The scene is laid?]. Many passages are powerful, especially the grave-digging [Is grave-digging a passage?]. The character of Horatio is a noble fellow [conception] and the same is true of Ophelia [Ophelia a fellow?]. The drama takes place over several weeks. [The action covers a period of several weeks.]

Exercise:

1. The grizzly bear eats little during the winter, but lives by so much fat gathered during the summer.
2. Before entering college, my parents were confronted with my future as to what I should do after I was graduated from high school.
3. Learning to study is a very important step at college, and it is to this one thing that you can trace the cause of failure of many students.
4. Hospital wards may be either large or small. The large ward, which is cheaper as to nursing, may contain forty beds, usually foreigners and poor people of the city.

COMPLETENESS OF THOUGHT

5. The story of *The Houseboat on the Styx* is set forth in Hades on the river Styx. This is supposed to be one of the rivers of the underworld. It is written to take place about the present day.

Transitions

The state of mind of a writer is not the state of mind of his reader. The writer knows his ideas, and has spent much time with them. The reader meets these ideas for the first time, and must gather them in at a glance. The relation between two ideas may be clear to the writer, and not at all clear to the reader. Therefore,

8. **In passing from one thought to another, make the connection clear. If necessary, insert a word, a phrase, or even a sentence, to carry the reader safely across.**

Space transition needed: We were surprised to see a house in the distance, but we went to the door and knocked. [This sentence does not give a reader the effect of distance.]

Better: We were surprised to see a house in the distance. *But we hastened toward it with thoughts of a warm meal and a good lodging. We entered the yard,* and went up to the door, and knocked.

Exterior-interior transition needed: We noticed that the house was built of cobblestones. There was a broad window from which we could look out upon the small stream that dashed down the rocky hillside.

Better: We noticed that the house was built of cobblestones. *We went inside, and found that the living room was large and airy.* There was a broad window from which we could look

COMPLETENESS OF THOUGHT

out upon the small stream that dashed down the rocky hillside.

Cause transition lacking: The Romans were great road-builders. They wished to maintain their empire.

Better: The Romans were great road-builders, *because means of moving troops quickly were necessary* to the maintenance of their empire.

General-to-particular transition needed: Modern machinery often makes men its slaves. Last summer I worked for the Chandler Company. [This gap in thought occurs oftenest between the first two sentences of a paragraph or theme.]

Better: Modern machinery often makes men its slaves. *This truth is well illustrated by my own experience.* Last summer I worked for the Chandler Company.

Transition to be improved by changing order: A careless trainer may spoil a good colt. A good horse can never be made of a vicious colt. [Here the order of ideas is: "Trainer . . . colt. Horse . . . colt." Turn the last sentence end for end.]

Better: A careless trainer may spoil a good colt. And a vicious colt can never be made a good horse. [Now the order of ideas is "Trainer . . . colt. Colt . . . horse."]

Transition to be improved by removal of a disturbing element: Our class in physics last week visited a pumping station in which the Corliss type of steam engine is used. *The engines are manufactured by the Allis-Chalmers Company of Milwaukee, Wisconsin.* This type of engine is used because it has several advantages. [The italicized sentence should be omitted here, and introduced later.]

The simplest means of securing smooth transitions is by a liberal use of connectives: *however, on the other hand, equally important, another interesting problem is, for this reason, the remedy for this, so much for, it remains to mention, of course I admit, finally.* (For a

COMPLETENESS OF THOUGHT

longer list see 36.) Such phrases are useful not only in linking sentences, but also in joining one paragraph to another. They are almost always necessary when there is a turn, a reversal, or a repetition of thought.

Note.—When a student first learns the art, he is likely to use transition phrases in excess, and produce something like the following: "When I have to write a theme, I first think of my subject. As soon as I have my subject, I take out my paper. On the paper I then make a rough outline." This abuse of transition results in an overlapping of thought, like shingles laid three inches to the weather. An abrupt transition is better than wordiness.

Exercise:
1. Mrs. Hicks neglects her household work. She has fireless cookers, vacuum cleaners, and all such conveniences.
2. Alden was susceptible to drafts. He put many windows in the house he was building.
3. A long vacation is not conducive to study. Last August I was in the mountains of Vermont.
4. Many men are leaving school just now. The Canadian government is sending out a call for men to work on farms is the reason.
5. I was pleased with my first glimpse of the house, set in spacious lawn and gardens. The fireplace was flanked with great bookcases full of books. This pleased me most of all.

COMPLETENESS OF THOUGHT

9. EXERCISE IN COMPLETENESS OF THOUGHT

A. Fragments Misused as Sentences

Rewrite the following statements in sentences each of which expresses a complete thought.

1. That evening he and I took a walk about the city. After which we returned to our room.
2. The water is clear and one can see the bottom at a depth of six feet. Or even ten feet.
3. The clerk made thirty sales yesterday. Thus far today only three.
4. Milk is carefully inspected nowadays. Especially if it is to be used by children.
5. The best colors for window draperies are tan, buff, gray, blue, and rose. My preference being for blue.
6. She was an unusually good cook of buckwheat cakes. As well as of waffles.
7. The train was an hour late. So that Baker missed the first act of the play.
8. She bought a hat for eighteen dollars. Whereas she meant to buy one for ten.
9. It was seen that the hit was a long one. That it would clear the right-field fence.
10. The cobbler put a patch on one side of the heel. Where the leather was worn off.
11. He preferred to drink water. Although coffee was served with the meal free.
12. Place the bread sponge to rise overnight. In a place where it will keep warm.
13. He remembered that night on the prairie. When the coyotes had howled round their camp.
14. There were three other rooms downstairs, perhaps smaller than the front room, but in the same style. The main difference being in the color of the walls, which were brown.

COMPLETENESS OF THOUGHT

15. I was greatly impressed by the trees and gardens about the campus. Also by the brilliant colors of the woodbine which climbs on the side of Quincy Hall.

B. Incomplete Constructions

Improve the following statements. Supply missing words. Make sure that each construction and each sentence is complete.

1. She pays more attention to her neighbors' business than her children.
2. A man reading these meters would take him ten hours' time or more.
3. Nor are these Yellowstone cliffs less wonderful in form than color.
4. Just what my profession is to be I have not made a final decision.
5. The farm needed laborers. So he asked the dean to get out of school.
6. The certainty that winter was at hand, he filled his coal bins with fuel.
7. It was an affront which he had difficulty to find the reason.
8. The women always had maids and plenty servants to do the work.
9. Smoke poured from the flue and also the window.
10. If a person lacks social training, although well dressed, will not be at ease at a reception.
11. Do you recall that in the conversation in which he declared he was familiar with every branch of civil engineering?
12. Although the light is dim is not proof that the battery is worn out.
13. A complicated business forces a man to make decisions that he can't stop to explain. This fact should be borne in mind, and not be too ready to call the man domineering.

COMPLETENESS OF THOUGHT

14. Bacon contrasts public and private envy by saying that there is no good in private envy, while in public there is much good.
15. By the time the jam reached the falls, which were a mile down the river, it had grown until layer after layer of ice, heaping one upon the other, with trees and driftwood holding them together.

C. Incomplete Logic

The following sentences are inadequate statements of cause, comparison, etc. Complete the thought.

1. The purpose and outlook of Andrew Jackson were different from preceding presidents.
2. That fellow's skin is thicker than a mule.
3. Kent was the most popular of all the other candidates.
4. Because he wore overshoes kept his feet warm.
5. A squad is where eight men form a military unit.
6. Chess requires deep and earnest study is the secret of its fascination for him.
7. His appetite is greater than an ostrich.
8. Nonchalant is where a person is indifferent.
9. Indirect lighting is when the light from the lamps is cast up to the ceiling and reflected down.
10. His wife's name was Helen and a blond.
11. Where the cars run underground is the definition of a subway.
12. The scholarship of the athletes in our school is above many of the other branches of school activity.
13. The ideas of Prospero are in some instances Shakespeare himself.
14. The man with wet shoes will burn the leather quicker than dry shoes.
15. Our legislators began to think of giving the children of the West the same educational advantages as the East.

COMPLETENESS OF THOUGHT

D. Undeveloped Thought and Transitions

Complete the thought of the following sentences, and secure a smooth transition between parts.

1. As you look back over history, many great nations have fallen.
2. Napoleon was an extraordinary military genius. Wellington defeated him.
3. In reply to no income, he said there had been a seven per cent dividend to the holders of all stock, preferred or common.
4. Those who seek to uplift the masses do not always have their ideas accepted eagerly. Last summer I worked in the slums of Boston.
5. His farm was well stocked with horses and mules. He had steam tractors and gasoline motors.
6. The work about the machinery was dangerous. Chamberlain had never been hurt.
7. Throughout life Franklin was a reformer. He wore the ordinary clothes common in his day.
8. Some large potatoes must be placed in the coals; likewise the coffee. Then you are ready to eat, as soon as the steak is fried.
9. Marken is a very small island. Thousands of tourists visit it. The costumes and manners of old Holland are seen to best advantage there.
10. Tungsten resists heat. The carbon-filament lamps were short lived. Some time later the tungsten-filament lamp was invented. These lamps are now universally used, because of their long life.

UNITY OF THOUGHT

Unity means oneness. A sentence should contain one thought. It may contain two or more statements only when these are closely related parts of a larger thought or impression. A writer should make certain, first, that his thought has unity; and second, that this unity will be obvious to the reader.

Independent Ideas in One Sentence

10. Do not combine ideas which have no obvious relation to each other. Do not combine ideas which *are* related if each is important enough to form a sentence by itself. (See 41.)

Wrong: The Spartans did not care for literature, and lived in the southern part of Greece.

Wrong: The coffee business is not difficult to learn, and the most important work in preparing the coffee for the market is the roasting of the green berries.

The simplest method of correction is to divide the sentence.

Right: The Spartans lived in the southern part of Greece. They did not care for literature.

Right: The coffee business is not difficult to learn. The most important work in preparing the coffee for the market is the roasting of the green berries.

Another method of correction is to subordinate one idea to the other, or to change the wording until the relation between the ideas is obvious. In instances where this method cannot be applied, the only remedy is to divide the sentence.

UNITY OF THOUGHT

Right: The Spartans, who lived in the southern part of Greece, did not care for literature.

Right: The coffee business is not difficult to learn, since the only important work in preparing the coffee for the market is the roasting of the green berries.

The following example presents three ideas:
> Idea 1—Ten years elapse.
> Idea 2—A man dies.
> Idea 3—A family moves.

These ideas are closely related. But at least two of the ideas are independent; that is to say, important enough to demand separate sentences.

Lacking unity: We lived in Santa Fé for ten years; then my father died, so we moved to El Paso, Texas.

Right [emphasizing ideas 2 and 3]: After we had lived in Santa Fé for ten years, my father died. We then moved to El Paso, Texas.

Right [emphasizing ideas 1 and 3]: We lived in Santa Fé for ten years. Upon the death of my father, the family moved to El Paso, Texas.

Exercise:
1. Houston was extremely fond of game fishing, and once he forgot to put out his camp fire.
2. His car was freshly painted, and he was wondering about his supply of gasoline.
3. We followed a narrow path up to the stone quarry; I often wondered how building stone was obtained.
4. The next morning he came across a herd of cattle; near by was a farmhouse, and he talked to the owner.
5. Putting on a bandage requires a degree of skill which is attained only after considerable practice; a properly applied bandage should be neither too tight nor too loose, and should remain in place twenty-four hours without readjustment.

UNITY OF THOUGHT

Excessive Detail

11. Do not encumber the main idea of a sentence with superfluous details. Place some of the details in another sentence, or omit them.

Faulty: In the town in which I live there are several large churches, and about six o'clock one morning, in a violent storm, one of these churches was struck by lightning.

Right: In my home town there are several large churches. One morning about six o'clock, in a violent storm, one of these churches was struck by lightning.

Wrong: In 1836, in Baltimore, Poe married Virginia Clemm, his cousin, who was hardly more than a child, being then fourteen years old, while Poe himself was twenty-eight, and to her he wrote much of his best verse.

Right: In 1836 Poe married Virginia Clemm. Poe was then twenty-eight, and Virginia was only fourteen. To this girl Poe wrote much of his best verse.

Exercise:

1. I arrived at Pana, Illinois, on a gasoline motor car, the kind that run on railroad tracks, with all my packages, and fifteen cents in my pocket, at twelve o'clock at night.
2. The house was ablaze, with hysterical people about, and great flames leaping upward, and very dense smoke, and all the goods of the household were being destroyed, for the village had no fire department.
3. Early on the third of July eight of us, in four canoes, with bedding and a week's provisions, not to mention tents, mosquito nets, fishing tackle, and two dogs, started on a trip through the Thousand Islands.
4. August is the month of rainy afternoons in the mountains, and I remember well the drenching I received last summer while in the Sierras, where I had gone with my uncle, who is a great fisherman, and a jolly companion.

UNITY OF THOUGHT

5. Palmer was in his first year at college, to which he had gone straight from the farm, when he learned through a friend of a great banking firm which, so his friend told him, would train bright young men at its own cost, and later have them represent it at good salaries in South America.

Stringy Sentences to be Broken up

12. Avoid stringy compound sentences. The crude, rambling style which results from their use may be corrected by separating the material into shorter sentences, or by subordinating lesser ideas to the main thought.

Faulty: The second speaker had sat quietly waiting, and he was a man of a different type, and he began calmly, yet from the very first words he showed great earnestness.

Right: The second speaker, who had sat quietly waiting, was a man of a different type. He began calmly, yet from his very first words he showed great earnestness.

Faulty: There are many stops on the organ which control the tones of the different pipes and one has to learn how and when to use these and this takes time and practice.

Right: On the organ are many stops which control the tones of the different pipes. To learn how and when to use these takes time and practice.

Faulty: He published prose fiction, and this was then the accepted literary form, and the drama was neglected.

Better: He published prose fiction, which was then the accepted literary form, the drama being neglected. [This sentence makes three statements in a diminishing series. The important idea is expressed in a main clause; a less important explanation is fitted into a relative clause; and a still less important comment takes a parenthetical phrase at the end.]

Note.—One of the crying faults of the immature writer is that by excessive coördination he obscures the fine

UNITY OF THOUGHT

shades of meaning. When two clauses are joined, the meaning will very often be more exact if one is subordinated to the other. For a list of subordinating connectives, see 36.

Exercise:
1. He dressed and ate breakfast and caught a car and reached the office and took his seat at the desk.
2. He bought the lots and simply held them while the neighborhood built up, and he refused to be frightened by the panic and became a rich man.
3. The first few cartoons were hard to make, but when he had his series fairly started, his troubles ended, and ideas for new cartoons came to him unsought, and subscribers even sent in suggestions as to what they would like.
4. There were various factions—the king's, the queen's, and Cardinal Richelieu's in particular—and D'Artagnan was one of the king's musketeers, but nevertheless he rendered great service to the queen, and Richelieu tried to bribe him with a lieutenancy but he refused it.
5. I measured one cup of rice into a pan, but that did not appear to be nearly enough for three people, so I promptly added two more, and it swelled and cooked and swelled again, and the final result was that we had rice pudding, rice croquettes, and rice everything for one week.

Choppy Sentences to be Combined

13. Do not use two or three short sentences to express ideas which will make a more unified impression in one sentence. Place subordinate ideas in subordinate grammatical constructions.

Excessive predication: Excavating is the first operation in street paving. The excavating is usually done by means of a steam shovel. The shovel scoops up the dirt and loads it directly into wagons.

UNITY OF THOUGHT

Right: Excavating, the first operation in street paving, is usually done by a steam shovel which loads the dirt directly into wagons.

Monotonous: The doe is wading along the shore. She is nibbling the lily pads as she goes. Now she moves slowly around the point. She has a little spotted fawn with her. The fawn frolics along at the heels of his mother.

Better: Wading along the shore, the doe nibbles the lily pads by the way, and moves slowly around the point. A spotted fawn frolics at her heels.

Primer style: Rooms are marked on the floor. These rooms are about fourteen feet square.

Better: The floor is marked off into rooms about fourteen feet square.

Note.—An occasional short sentence is permissible, even desirable. Successive short sentences may be used to express rapid action, or emphatic assertion, or deliberate simplicity. Otherwise, avoid them.

Exercise:

1. This watch has a radium face. The radium face enables the owner to see the time in the dark.
2. In a ravine not far from the house was a spring. A narrow path led to this spring through the willows.
3. Throughout New England the elms were being destroyed. The destruction was caused by moths. These moths were not native to the country. The moths, on the contrary, had come from abroad.
4. The mail is brought in by automobile. It arrives about two o'clock. Everybody gathers at the post office. It is like a social gathering. Every one knows every one else.
5. The boat stopped short in the fog. We felt an icy blast of wind. Then we saw an iceberg towering above us. We waited for it to float past. Then a little berg came into sight. I remarked to the captain that it wasn't even a

UNITY OF THOUGHT

quarter's worth. "But it has roots," he said. "Not like a politician—all on the surface."

Excessive Coördination

In structure a sentence may be

A. Simple: The rain fell.
B. Compound: The rain continued and the stream rose.
C. Complex: When the rain ceased, the flood came.

In B, the clauses are of almost equal importance, and the first is coördinated with the second. In C, the clauses are not of equal importance, and the first is subordinated to the second. *And* is a coördinating conjunction. *When* is a subordinating conjunction. For a list of connectives see 36.

14. Do not use coördination when subordination will secure a more clear and emphatic unit of thought. Especially do not coördinate a main idea with an explanatory detail. Children connect all ideas, important and unimportant, with *and;* discriminating writers place minor ideas in subordinate clauses, consign still less important ideas to participial or prepositional phrases, and omit trivial details altogether.

Childish: I went down town and saw a crowd standing in the street, and wanted to know what was the matter, and so I went up and asked a man.
Right: When I went down town, I saw a crowd standing in the street, and since I wanted to know what was the matter, I asked a man. [Two clauses are subordinated by the use of

UNITY OF THOUGHT

when and *since*. This change abolishes two *ands*. The words *went up and* are struck out. One *and* remains, and deserves to remain, for it joins two ideas which are truly coördinate.]

Main idea not emphasized: I talked with an old man and his name was Ned.

Better: I talked with an old man named Ned. [A participial phrase replaces a clause. The name is now subordinated.]

Main idea not emphasized: Developing is the next step in preparing the film, and it is very important.

Better: Developing, the next step in preparing the film, is very important. [An appositional phrase replaces the first predicate.]

Main idea not emphasized: They began their perilous journey, and they had four horses.

Right [emphasizing *perilous journey*]: With four horses they began their perilous journey. [A prepositional phrase replaces a clause.]

Right [emphasizing *having the horses*]: When they began their perilous journey, they had four horses. [A subordinate clause replaces a main clause.]

Capable of greater unity: The frog is a stupid animal, and may be caught with a hook baited with red flannel. [Is the writer trying to tell us *how to catch frogs* or merely that *frogs are stupid?* Coördination makes the two ideas appear equally important.]

Right [emphasizing *frogs are stupid*]: The fact that the frog can be caught with a hook baited with red flannel proves his stupidity.

Right [emphasizing *how to catch frogs*]: The frog, being stupid, will bite at a piece of red flannel.

Exercise:

1. Many committees have been appointed, and the one on finance is the most important, and Sherrill is chairman of it.
2. A great storm arose, and the boatmen decided that Jonah must be the cause of the storm, and they threw him overboard, and then the storm ceased.

UNITY OF THOUGHT

3. It was a little mountain stream, and it bubbled along happily and I was captivated, and I decided to follow it, and to find where it went.
4. The walls of the room are of cardboard, and they are painted gray. None of the houses in the village are very large, but contain only two or three rooms, and they are never more than one story in height.
5. Pharaoh saw that Joseph was a discreet man, and made him food administrator, and during the seven years of plenty, Joseph traveled over the country and urged the people to plant more corn, and, when the harvest was ready, to store it in great quantities throughout Egypt, and in this way the people might have plenty to eat during the years of famine which were to come.

Faulty Subordination of the Main Thought

15. Do not put the principal statement of a sentence in a subordinate clause or phrase. This violation of unity is sometimes called "upside-down subordination" (See 42).

Faulty: Our clothes began to feel damp from the fog, when we decided to build a fire.

Right: When our clothes began to feel damp from the fog, we decided to build a fire.

Faulty: Longstreet received orders to attack the Federal right wing, which he did immediately.

Right: As soon as Longstreet received orders, he attacked the Federal right wing.

Faulty: I suspected that it would rain, although I did not take an umbrella.

Right: Although I suspected that it would rain, I did not take an umbrella.

Exercise:

1. The chill of November was in the air, when we decided it was a good time to kill hogs.

UNITY OF THOUGHT

2. We had driven in a wedge, although the wood still pinched the saw.
3. He replied to the charge, pleading not guilty.
4. General Tilney asks Catherine to visit their home, Northanger Abbey, which she does.
5. The two teams fought hard, while fortune seemed to favor Chicago.

Subordination Thwarted by *and*

16. Do not attach to a main clause by means of *and*, a word, phrase, or clause which you intend shall be subordinate. The presence of *and* thwarts subordination.

Wrong: Major went to bed, and leaving the work unfinished.
Right: Major went to bed, leaving the work unfinished.
Wrong: He ran home and with coat tails flying.
Right: He ran home with coat tails flying.

Exercise:

1. He rebuked them, and harshly. He was brighter than I, and in many ways.
2. She made her way at last through the huge stack of papers, and thus completing her day's work. She folded and put away the letter, and talking all the while.
3. James next writes a chapter on "Habit", and showing how many of our daily actions are performed involuntarily.
4. When I confronted him with the evidence, his face grew red, and thus indicating his guilt.
5. He saw a crow's nest in the top of the tree, and where a stroke of lightning had split away half of the limb.

The *and which* construction

17. Use *and which* (or *but which*), and *who* (or *but who*) only between relative clauses similar in form. Be-

UNITY OF THOUGHT

tween a main clause and a relative clause, *and* or *but* thwarts subordination.

Wrong: This is an important problem, and which we shall not find easy to solve.
Right: This is an important problem, which we shall not find easy to solve.
Right: This problem is one *which* is important, *and which* we cannot easily solve.
Wrong: *Les Miserables* is a novel of great interest and which everybody should read.
Right: *Les Miserables* is a novel of great interest, and one which everybody should read.
Wrong: Their chief opponent was Winter, a shrewd politician, but who is now less popular than he was.
Right: Their chief opponent was Winter, a shrewd politician, who is now less popular than he was.

Note.—Rule 17 is sometimes briefly stated: "Do not use *and which* unless you have already used *which* in the sentence." This statement is generally true, but an exception must be made for sentences like the following: Right: "He told me what countries he had visited, and which ones he liked most."

Exercise:
1. The cashier promised to save the foreign stamps, and which would make his collection more varied.
2. All normal people have ambitions but which are not achieved.
3. He is a man of the utmost good nature, but who never pays his bills.
4. The girl in the blue dress, and whom we had seen at the station, was his employer's niece.
5. His shoulder had suffered a strain, but which some witch hazel relieved.

UNITY OF THOUGHT

Unity Thwarted by Punctuation
The Comma Splice

8. **Do not splice two independent statements by means of a comma. Write two sentences. Or, if the two statements together form a unit of thought, combine them (1) by a comma plus a conjunction, (2) by a semicolon, or (3) by reducing one of the statements to a phrase or a subordinate clause.**

Wrong: The town has two railroads, it was founded when oil was discovered.

Right: The town has two railroads. It was founded when oil was discovered.

Wrong: The speed of the car seemed slower than it really was, this was due, no doubt, to the absence of all noise. [Here are three commas. The reader cannot quickly discover which one marks the great division of thought.]

Right: The speed of the car seemed slower than it really was. This was due, no doubt, to the absence of all noise.

Wrong: The winters were long and cold, nothing could live without shelter.

Right: The winters were long and cold. Nothing could live without shelter.

Right: The winters were long and cold, and nothing could live without shelter [For the use of the comma, see 91a].

Right: The winters were long and cold; nothing could live without shelter [For the use of the semicolon see 92].

Right: The winters were so long and cold that nothing could live without shelter.

Exception.—Short coördinate clauses which are parallel in structure and leave a unified impression, may be joined by commas, even though the conjunctions be omitted.

UNITY OF THOUGHT

Right: All was excitement. The ducks quacked, the pigs squealed, the dogs barked. [The general idea *excitement* gives the three clauses a certain unity.]

Exercise:

1. Ralston shivered, it was very cold.
2. The Indians did not live as the cliff-dwellers did, they wandered about instead of dwelling in a village.
3. In one corner of the garden sunflowers blossomed, in another corner hollyhocks had their own way.
4. There is in food a quality called "vitamines" which produces growth, if the food is cooked too long this quality is destroyed.
5. He asked in vain at the hardware store, at the furniture store, at the department store, and at the second-hand store, by good luck, he found it.

19. EXERCISE IN UNITY OF THOUGHT

A. The Comma Splice

Rewrite the following material in sentences each of which is a unit of thought. Most of the statements should be summarily cut apart. If you decide that others taken together have unity of thought, combine them (1) by a comma plus a conjunction, (2) by a semicolon, or (3) by reducing one of the statements to a phrase or a subordinate clause.

1. His temperature had risen, it was now 104.
2. Some of these candidates he accepts, some he rejects.
3. Glance about you, notice the weeds growing in the streets.
4. The Crusaders went forth to enforce their ideas with spear and blade, they came back carrying new ideas in their heads.
5. I am always interested in you and your work, do write to me again.

UNITY OF THOUGHT

6. We wished to dig the Panama Canal, we had first to destroy the mosquitoes.
7. They remain here for several years to make money, then they return to China.
8. The cold is intense, one does not suffer from it much because the atmosphere is dry.
9. This house remained my home until I was five years old, then we moved to a town twenty miles away.
10. And of course they lived happily ever after, at least, we hope so.
11. One of the cabins is used to cook and eat in, the other is used to sleep in.
12. I began selling milk to three families, in time I had a large number of customers.
13. The key turns slowly in the rusty lock, the lid lifts.
14. Woman's dress in this period was queer, bustles were worn, and the skirts were draped long and dragged the floor.
15. During the fifteenth and sixteenth centuries the Indes had been reached, the ancient world with its treasures, knowledge, and literature had been rediscovered.

B. One Thought in a Sentence

By dividing, subordinating, or logically combining the following statements, secure unity of thought.

1. The Chinese have slant eyes and subsist largely on rice.
2. Walsh was a kind-hearted fellow and was wet to the skin.
3. Irene, being twenty-seven years old, was a brunette.
4. This section was noted for its apples, and the farmers had to spray the trees carefully.
5. I entered the third grade; the teacher would not allow me to take books from the library.
6. Stanley Park in Vancouver is filled with great trees. These trees are hundreds of years old.
7. The box was four feet long. It was three feet wide. It was two and a half feet high.

UNITY OF THOUGHT

8. Caruso was the son of poor parents and possessed a magnificent tenor voice.
9. Robbins was the night editor and had won first place in the chess tournament.
10. The nobles were Norman in blood, and hunting and hawking were their favorite amusements.
11. Turner has a hook nose and works in a foundry; his people are reputed to be very rich.
12. He bought the lumber. Then he hauled it here. The two-by-fours were sound. But the one-by-six boards were full of knot holes.
13. After you have selected a sunny place for your garden, purchase a rake, hoe, spade, and the seed, and prepare the soil by turning it over carefully with the spade and raking it smooth with the rake, after which plant the seed and water the plot daily for ten days.
14. We have received your complaint and assure you that the articles were in good condition when they were shipped, but we shall replace them with sound merchandise and ourselves collect from the carriers, and we trust this solution is satisfactory to you.

C. Excessive Coördination

The ideas in the following sentences are loosely strung together with coördinating conjunctions. Place the important idea in the main clause. Subordinate other ideas by reducing each to a dependent clause, or a phrase, or a word.

1. Killibrew was the next man to speak, and he was chairman of the finance committee.
2. He kept a cigar in his mouth, but without lighting it.
3. The Romans won the naval battle, and the Carthaginians no longer commanded the sea.
4. She gave me a cup of tea, and there was lemon in it.

UNITY OF THOUGHT

5. He had on a new hat and it was a tall silk one and seemed very strange to the villagers.
6. He made up the deficit, and out of his own resources.
7. Kate had a guardian, and he allowed her less spending money than she wanted.
8. The engineers are planning a new bridge, and which will carry street cars as well as wagon traffic.
9. Between the layers of the cake were the fillings, and these were of chocolate, and there were two of them.
10. We had been on the road for an hour, and we were riding along in a canyon that had steep sides, and we heard a rumbling noise ahead.
11. The other day I saw a group of men talking, and I walked up to them, and found that the topic of conversation was cheating.
12. There was one bright patch of color—the calendar the grocer's boy had presented me with, and which hung on the kitchen wall.
13. Thus we splashed along the road, and our wet skirts swished as we walked, and we were wet to the skin, yet we enjoyed it, and it was a new experience.
14. I was out in the wilds one day and saw a forest ranger, and I had always wondered what the life of such a man was like, and so I stopped him and we passed the time of day, and then I began to ask him questions.
15. My mother was a very courageous and self-reliant woman, and I remember one day when father was away she saw a tramp coming up the road and by the time he reached the door she had a towel around my head, and told the tramp that I had smallpox.

D. Excessive Predication

The following sentences are badly broken up. Rewrite them. Take care that you do not crowd too many ideas together, for stringy sentences are worse than choppy ones.

19
UNITY OF THOUGHT

1. To my right was a long stretch of sandy beach. This beach was dotted with bathers and loungers.
2. We found a stream at last. We followed it. It led out of this flat desert. We came to a broken country. The country was wooded, too.
3. Did you ever attend a country dance? If not, you have missed much. No one ever receives an invitation. You hear that there is to be a dance. You know that you will be welcome.
4. Then we went to the football field. This field, where all the university games are played, is known as Cummings' Field.
5. The Romans had many gods. If one god would not answer their prayers, they tried another. Sometimes there was an earthquake or a volcanic eruption. They thought these things represented the anger of the gods.
6. According to Thoreau we do not profit by the mistakes of others. It seems to me that this is true. We receive much good advice. But do we profit by it? As a rule we do not. We reason that we are different. We think we are as wise as our counselors.
7. I was tired of trying to keep a secret diary. I decided that I would stop trying to keep one. Some time later we moved away from that house. I left my diary in a glass jar under the steps. I suppose it is still there.
8. Smith became ill. His wife gave him medicine. He grew worse. They sent for the doctor. The doctor gave him more medicine. He grew worse still. They hired a trained nurse. This finished him. They sent for the undertaker. The undertaker didn't give him any medicine. Smith came back to life. The undertaker was angry. He too should have given Smith medicine.
9. *The Ambitious Guest* is a short tragedy. Its setting is the White Mountains. The family consists of the father and the mother, the grandmother, and the children. These are all seated around a warm fire. The grandmother is

UNITY OF THOUGHT

knitting. They are all the picture of health. They are talking together. A knock is heard at the door. A young man enters.

E. Upside-down Subordination

In the following sentences the important idea is buried in a subordinate clause or phrase. Rescue this main idea, express it in the main clause, and if possible subordinate the rest of the sentence to it.

1. The mouse nibbles the cheese, when the trap is sprung.
2. The package did not look dangerous, though it contained dynamite.
3. Cowan next took the stand, who denied any knowledge of the affair.
4. He followed the trail for hours, shooting a deer.
5. The car is geared low, climbing hills readily.
6. Matches went out as soon as ignited, thus showing that the air of the mine was foul and deadly.
7. He had a suspicion, which was that Jethro was the cause of the mischief.
8. Kane lives in our city, who has just been elected to the senate.
9. He waxed haughty, refusing all compromise.
10. This afternoon I was working in the laboratory when one of the boys spilled acid on his hand.
11. Magruder asked the routine questions, with no sign of recognition, although he looked me in the face.
12. In the fire Crusoe burnt the clay, thus making for himself several bowls and pitchers.
13. He made up his mind that he would speak to the butler about it, which he did.
14. He wrote me a letter on the subject, where he pointed out the fallacy of my assumption.
15. The children have gone to bed, and the older people are beginning to yawn, when suddenly a deafening roar is heard.

CLEARNESS OF THOUGHT

Clearness is fundamental. The writer should be content, not when his meaning may be understood, but only when his meaning cannot be misunderstood. He may attain this entire clearness by giving attention to five matters:

> Reference (20–23)
> Coherence (24–28)
> Parallel Structure (30–31)
> Consistency (32–35)
> Use of Connectives (36–38)

REFERENCE

By the use of pronouns, participles, and other dependent words, language becomes flexible and free. But each dependent part must refer without confusion to a word which is reasonably near, and properly expressed. Ordinarily a reader expects a pronoun or a participle to refer to the nearest noun (or pronoun) or to an emphatic noun.

Divided Reference

20. **A pronoun should be placed near the word to which it refers, and separated from words to which it might falsely seem to refer. If this method does not secure clearness, discard the pronoun and change the sentence structure.**

Uncertain reference of *which:* He dropped the bundle in the mud which he was carrying to his mother. [The reader for

CLEARNESS BY REFERENCE

a moment refers the pronoun to the wrong noun. Bring *which* nearer to its proper antecedent *bundle*.]

Right: He dropped in the mud the bundle which he was carrying to his mother.

Vague reference of *this:* My failure in mathematics was serious. My grades in English, history, and Latin were good enough. But this brought down my average. [*This?* What *this?* Five nouns intrude between the pronoun *this* and its proper antecedent *failure*.]

Right: In English, history, and Latin I received fairly good grades. But in mathematics I received a failure. This brought down my average.

Remote reference of *it:* If you want to make a good speech, take your hands out of your pockets, open your mouth wide, and throw yourself into it.

Right: If you want to make a good speech, take your hands out of your pockets, open your mouth wide, and throw yourself into what you are saying. [Or, better] Take your hands out of your pockets, open your mouth wide, and throw yourself into the speech.

Ambiguous reference of *he:* John spoke to the stranger, and he was very surly.

Right: John spoke to the stranger, who was very surly. [Or] John spoke in a surly manner to the stranger.

Note.—The reference of relative and demonstrative pronouns is largely dependent upon their position. The reference of a personal pronoun (*he, she, they,* etc.) is not so much dependent upon its position, the main consideration being that the antecedent shall be emphatic. (See the next article.)

Exercise:

1. I gave him a dollar for the dog which he said was too little.
2. Sears talked it over with McGrady, and he was very gracious about it.

CLEARNESS BY REFERENCE

3. The girls take lessons in painting with oils and water colors. These cost them considerable money.
4. Russia proposed to sell Alaska. By virtue of her geographical position she may be called the gateway to the North.
5. He took the grain to mill on an old mule which was then ground into flour. In pioneer days life was rough. Might made right. Now it is quite another thing.

Weak Reference

21. Do not allow a pronoun to refer to a word not likely to be central in the reader's thought; a word, for example, in the possessive case, or in a parenthetical expression, or in a compound, or not expressed at all. Make the pronoun refer to an emphatic word.

Wrong: When a poor woman came to Jane Addams' famous Hull House, she always gave help. [*Poor woman* and *Hull House* are the emphatic words, to which any pronoun used later is instinctively referred by the reader.]

Right: When a poor woman came to Jane Addams' famous Hull House, she always received help. [Or] When a poor woman came to Hull House, Jane Addams always gave help.

Wrong: In biology, which is the study of plants and animals, we find that they are made up of unitary structures called cells. [Since the words *plants and animals* occur only in a parenthetical clause, the reader is surprised to find them used as an antecedent.]

Right: In the study of biology we find that plants and animals are made up of unitary structures called cells.

Wrong: The old scissors-grinder sharpens them for the whole neighborhood. [The center of interest in the reader's mind is a man, not scissors.]

CLEARNESS BY REFERENCE

Right: This old scissors-grinder sharpens scissors for the whole neighborhood.

Wrong: I always liked engineers, and I have chosen that as my profession.
Right: I always liked engineering, and I have chosen it as my profession.

Absurd: When the baby is through drinking milk, it should be disconnected and put in boiling water. [The central idea in the reader's mind is *baby*, not *milk-bottle*. The writer may have been thinking about the *bottle*, but he did not make the word emphatic; in fact, he did not express it at all.]
Right: When the baby is through drinking milk, the bottle should be taken apart and put in boiling water.

Note.—Ordinarily, do not refer to the title in the first line of a theme. The reader expects you to assert something, and face forward, not to turn back to what you have said in the title.

Faulty: Color Photography
  I am interested in this new development of science. For a long time I . . .
Right: Color Photography
  Taking pictures in color has long appealed to me as an interesting possibility . . .

Exercise:
1. He threw a stone at the wasps' nest, which flew out angrily and stung him.
2. Washington was Braddock's aide-de-camp, who was surprised by the Indians and slain.
3. Daniel did not forget what he had been taught at home, and practiced them in Babylonia as well as in Palestine.
4. On Bastile Day the French, with great ceremony, buried one of her unknown dead under the Arc de Triomphe in Paris.

CLEARNESS BY REFERENCE

5. Along comes another tray, and the cashier will calculate his meal by checking it over, which will not cost him more than fifty cents.

Broad Reference

22. Do not use a pronoun to refer broadly to a general idea. Supply a definite antecedent or abandon the pronoun.

Wrong: The tapper strikes the gong, which continues as long as the push button is pressed. [The writer intends that *which* shall refer to the entire preceding clause, but the reference is intercepted by the word *gong*.]

Right [supplying a definite antecedent]: The tapper strikes the gong, a process which continues as long as the push button is pressed. [Or, abandoning the pronoun] The tapper strikes the gong as long as the push button is pressed.

Wrong: Read the directions which are printed on the bottle and it may save you from making a mistake.

Right [supplying a definite antecedent]: Read the directions which are printed on the bottle. This precaution may save you from making a mistake. [Or, abandoning the pronoun] Reading the directions on the bottle may prevent a mistake.

Wrong: The managers told him they would increase his salary if he would represent them in South America. He refused that.

Right: The managers told him they would increase his salary if he would represent them in South America. He refused the offer.

Exception.—It cannot be maintained that a pronoun must *always* have one definite word for its antecedent. Many of the best English authors occasionally use a pronoun to refer to a clause. But the reference must always be clear.

CLEARNESS BY REFERENCE

Note.—Impersonal constructions must be used with caution. "It is raining" is correct, although *it* has no antecedent. We desire that the antecedent shall be vague, impersonal. But unnecessary use of the indefinite *it, you,* or *they* should be avoided.

Faulty: It says in our history that Columbus was an Italian.
Right: Our history says that Columbus was an Italian.
Not complimentary to the reader: You aren't hanged nowadays for stealing.
Right: No one is hanged nowadays for stealing.
Faulty: They are noted for their tact in France.
Right: The French are noted for their tact.

Exercise:

1. He destroyed the vermin which made the place habitable.
2. The town has a library, a theater, two public schools, and four churches, which is unusual for such a small town.
3. The man said that, having worked in a slaughter house, it was proof enough he knew hides.
4. The automobile engine must have an efficient cooling system as well as a good lubricating system, which was not easy to perfect.
5. A deep foundation is necessary when a house rests upon "made" soil, and that is why the floors of Barlow's cabin were warped.

Dangling Participle or Gerund

23. A participle, being dependent, must refer to a noun or pronoun. The noun or pronoun should be within the sentence which contains the participle, and should be so conspicuous that the participle will be associated with it instantly and without confusion.

CLEARNESS BY REFERENCE

Wrong: Coming in on the train, the high school building is seen. [Is the building coming in? If not, who is?]
Right: Coming in on the train, one sees the high school building.

A sentence containing a dangling participle may be corrected (1) by giving the word to which the participle refers a conspicuous position in the sentence, or (2) by replacing the participial phrase by some other construction.

Wrong: Having taken our seats, the umpire announced the batteries.
Right: Having taken our seats, we heard the umpire announce the batteries. [Or] When we had taken our seats, the umpire announced the batteries.

Wrong: She was for a long time sick, caused by overwork. [The participle *caused* should not modify *sick*. A participle is used as an adjective, and should therefore modify a noun.]

Right — using an adjectival modifier:

She had a long sickness, $\begin{Bmatrix} \text{caused by} \\ \text{due to} \end{Bmatrix}$ overwork.

Right — using an adverbial modifier:

She was for a long time sick $\begin{Bmatrix} \text{because of} \\ \text{on account of} \end{Bmatrix}$ overwork.

When a gerund phrase *(in passing, by observing,* etc.) implies the action of a special agent, indicate what the agent is. Otherwise the phrase will be dangling.

Faulty: In talking to Mr. Brown the other day, he told me that you intend to buy a car.
Better: In talking to Mr. Brown the other day, I learned that you intend to buy a car.

CLEARNESS BY REFERENCE

Faulty: The address was concluded by reciting a passage from Wordsworth.
Better: The speaker concluded his address by reciting a passage from Wordsworth. [Or] The address was concluded by the recitation of a passage from Wordsworth.

Note.—Two other kinds of dangling modifier, treated elsewhere in this book, may be briefly mentioned here. A phrase beginning with the adjective *due* should refer to a noun; otherwise the phrase is left dangling (See 5 Note). An elliptical sentence (one from which words are omitted) is faulty when one of the elements is left dangling (See 3).

Faulty: I was late *due* to carelessness [Use *because of*].
Ludicrous: My shoestring always breaks when hurrying to the office at eight o'clock [Say *when I am hurrying*].

Exercise:
1. Going to a Hallowe'en party, two black cats crossed my path.
2. Facing straight ahead and southeast, the Squaw can be seen, and turning around, the red rock formation called the Papoose.
3. By following close behind the plow, the worms fall an easy prey to the robins.
4. Being very stupid, Robinson called the donkey Goop. On his left hand he had only three fingers, caused by an accident in his childhood.
5. Not climbing very fast, the top of the hill was still a long way off. Having arrived at the little grove they had selected, the baskets were set down. Scrambling upon a high rock, a river and three lakes could be seen.
6. In talking to a farmer, he said that he had secured a harvest only once in three years, produced by extremely dry weather.

CLEARNESS BY COHERENCE

COHERENCE

The verb *cohere* means to stick or hold firmly together. And the noun *coherence* as applied to writing means a close and natural sequence of parts. Order is essential to clearness.

General Incoherence

24. Every part of a sentence must have a clear and natural connection with the adjoining part. Like or related parts should normally be placed together.

Bring related ideas together: Little Helen stood beside the horse wearing white stockings and slippers.
Right: Little Helen, in white stockings and slippers, stood beside the horse.
Keep unlike ideas apart: The colors of purple and green are pleasing to the eye as found in the thistle.
Right: The purple and green colors of the thistle are pleasing.
Distribute unrelated modifiers, instead of bunching them: I found   a heap of snow   on my bed   in the morning   which had drifted in through the window. [Subject verb — object — place — time — explanation.]
Right: In the morning   I found   on my bed   a heap of snow   which had drifted in through the window. [Time — subject verb — place — object — explanation.]
Bring related modifiers together: When he has prepared his lessons, he will come, as soon as he can put on his old clothes. [Condition — main clause — condition.]
Right: When he has prepared his lessons and put on his old clothes, he will come. [Condition and condition — main clause.]

Exercise:
1. I first saw the house from a steamer where I afterward lived for seven years.

CLEARNESS BY COHERENCE

2. She was the widow of a well-known lawyer, prominent in society and in philanthropic work.
3. Our next task was to transport the wood that we had found up the hill.
4. He could see the ocean on his left through a rift in the mountains where a ship was in full sail.
5. You can always find a crowd around the cages of the monkeys at the zoo on a summer afternoon at Washington.

Logical Sequence

25. Place first in the sentence the idea which naturally comes first in thought or in the order of time.

Faulty: We went to the station from the house after bidding all goodby.
Right: We said goodby to all, and went from the house to the station.

Ordinarily, let a second thought begin where the first leaves off.

Faulty: An orange grove requires plenty of water. The young trees will die if they do not have plenty of water. [The order of ideas is: "Grove ... water. Trees ... water." Reverse the order of the second sentence.]
Right: An orange grove requires plenty of water. For without water the young trees will die. [Now the order of ideas is: "Grove ... water. Water ... trees."]

Do not begin one idea, abandon it for a second, and then return to the first. Complete one idea at a time.

Faulty: Once, while hunting, the king was caught in a rain storm. He gave two old peasants who lived in a windmill rings and fine clothing, and made them very rich. These people did him a kindness, offering him shelter and warm food, when he took refuge there from the storm, in order to escape a drenching.

CLEARNESS BY COHERENCE

Right: Once, while hunting, the king was caught in a rain storm. In order to escape a drenching he took refuge in a windmill. The two old peasants who lived there were kind, offering him shelter and warm food. Whereupon the king gave them rings and fine clothing, and made them very rich.

Exercise:
1. Lincoln was reëlected. He thought in the early stages of the campaign that he would be defeated.
2. Down to the present time, there have always been in the world great religious leaders, one inspiring the other, from Dwight L. Moody back to Moses.
3. At last he got into the old house, and here he saw only a lot of dusty furniture. He had unlocked the door with a skeleton key.
4. I drove into the country fourteen miles to apply for a school, having donned clothes which I thought were most severe and formal.
5. We are in a hurry to finish the survey, but now the chainman has lost his plumb-bob. This instrument is found about a mile back under a pine tree, after we have searched carefully for it for an hour.

Squinting Modifier

26. Avoid the squinting construction. That is, do not place between two parts of a sentence a modifier that may attach itself to either. Place the modifier where it cannot be misunderstood.

Confusing: I told him when the time came I would do it. [*When the time came* is said to "squint" because the reader cannot tell whether it looks forward to the end of the sentence, or backward to the beginning.]
Right: When the time came, I told him I would do it. [Or] I told him I would do it when the time came.

CLEARNESS BY COHERENCE

Confusing: Some friends I knew would enjoy the play. [*I knew* squints.]
Right: Some friends would enjoy the play, I knew.
Confusing: The orator whom every one was calling for enthusiastically hurried to the platform. [*Enthusiastically* squints.]
Clear: The orator whom every one was enthusiastically calling for hurried to the platform.

Exercise:

1. He said after a minute he would go.
2. The man whom she addressed unceremoniously came toward her.
3. After the pottery is shaped in two hours it goes to the kiln.
4. Being dishonest ninety-nine times in a hundred does not pay.
5. I have tried to sketch the plan I had in view when the article was written on the opposite page.

Misplaced Word

27. Such an adverb as *only, ever, almost,* should be placed near the word it modifies, and separated from words which it might falsely seem to modify. Such a conjunction as *nevertheless,* if required with a clause, should usually be placed near the beginning.

Illogical: I only need a few dollars.
Right: I need only a few dollars.
Illogical: I don't ever intend to go there again.
Right: I don't intend ever to go there again. [Or] I intend never to go there again.
Illogical: She has the sweetest voice I nearly ever heard.
Right: She has nearly [or *almost*] the sweetest voice I ever heard.

CLEARNESS BY COHERENCE

Tardy use of conjunction: I intend to try. I do not expect to accomplish much, however.

Right: I intend to try. I do not, however, expect to accomplish much.

Exercise:

1. It was the best piece of sirloin he had almost ever eaten.
2. Many farmers will only plant their crops under a certain phase of the moon.
3. The thermometer stood at zero. We decided, after talking the matter over, that we would not wear our fur coats, however.
4. That was one piece of folly he never intended to be guilty of.
5. It is only necessary to irrigate the fields in July and August, and then even the ground can be kept moist if only watered every ten days.

Split Construction

28. Elements that have a close grammatical connection should not be separated awkwardly or carelessly. These elements are: (a) subject and verb, or verb and object; (b) the parts of a compound verb; and (c) the parts of an infinitive.

Awkward: One in the struggle for efficiency should not become a machine.

Better: In the struggle for efficiency one should not become a machine.

Awkward: What use of an education could a girl who married a penniless rogue and afterwards knew nothing but hard labor, make?

Better: What use of an education could a girl make who married a penniless rogue and afterward knew nothing but hard labor?

Crude: He was unable to even so much as stir a foot.

Better: He was unable even to stir a foot.

CLEARNESS BY COHERENCE

Note.—It is often desirable to separate the forms enumerated under (a) and (b) above, either for emphasis (See 40) or to avoid a bunching of modifiers at the end of a sentence (See 24). The whole point of rule 28 is not to depart from a natural order needlessly.

Exercise:
1. You should, instead of sitting at the desk dreaming, act.
2. The glare of the fire seemed to completely and powerfully light the city.
3. Cady, as the fullback caught the ball for the punt, lunged forward to tackle him.
4. He climbed into the rigging and shouted, for the wind had grown very strong, his answer.
5. It is not wise to plant fruit trees on a lawn, for much water will, though necessary to keep the grass green and flourishing, stunt or even kill them.

9. EXERCISE IN CLEARNESS OF THOUGHT

A. Reference of Pronouns

In the following sentences make the reference of pronouns exact and unmistakable.

1. He handed the cashier a personal check after giving him a satisfactory bank draft that could not be cashed.
2. The rooms are cold and cheerless, but they are the homes of New York's tenement people, and they never whimper.
3. The opposing lawyer tried to persuade him that the matter should be settled out of court for a small sum. He scorned this.
4. I have a hearty appetite for dinner which is lacking if I do not have some outdoor exercise.
5. He refused to put in an application which might cause him to lose the appointment.

CLEARNESS OF THOUGHT

6. Jackson gave Hendricks legal notice that he could not occupy the apartment after the first of the month.
7. Norah was frying an egg in a skillet that had two yolks.
8. Trains move at such speed that our continent can be crossed in four days, which formerly took months.
9. In medieval cathedrals, where strange, artistic figures were carved by leisurely monks, we oftentimes see them in a fine state of preservation.
10. The children's hair was slicked back tight from their faces which had been combed and brushed repeatedly.
11. Frank could not fire, because the bear was trying to climb the tree, and he shook the tree so much that he could not take aim.
12. He was very weak and pale after his return from the arctic regions, which made the scar on his cheek the more red and disfiguring.
13. People usually make resolutions on New Year's Day; but they do not need to wait until that time to make them, because they can be made by them any day.
14. Another objection to a fraternity is their idea that they are above the ordinary intelligence of students. This is not true of every fraternity man, but a good many of them have this idea.
15. The house where we lived was twelve blocks from the street car line, which ran only every hour. This kept my mother in the house a great deal during the winter snows, which became very tiresome to her.

B. Dangling Modifiers

Remembering that a participle is used as an adjective and must therefore refer to a noun or pronoun, correct the following sentences. Gerund phrases and a few elliptical sentences are included in the list.

1. Looking from the Cliff House out upon the ocean, a huge rock could be seen.

CLEARNESS OF THOUGHT

2. After thinking about it for a few minutes, his finger pressed the button.
3. Entering the room, a great brick fireplace catches the eye.
4. His hat came off while hurrying to catch a car.
5. Sitting tense in gallery, parquet, and box seats, the great actor spoke the celebrated lines.
6. Striking at it furiously with a board, the dog dropped the chicken it had seized.
7. Coming up for the third time, struggling, strangling, Hicks threw him a life preserver that lay on the deck.
8. The door bell rang when hoeing weeds in the back yard.
9. Glancing out over the valley, twenty-eight lakes could be counted.
10. The horse had only one good eye, caused by an encounter with a wire fence.
11. Settling back in her chair, her knitting needles clicked busily.
12. A hundred and seven words were written in one minute, using every finger in striking the keys.
13. When wound up, you will not have to bother with the clock again for a week.
14. The bus holds fifteen people, and being full, the bus man shuts the door.
15. Not being gifted with a singing voice, the phonograph came in handy in my school room.

C. Coherence

Secure a clear, smooth, natural order for the following sentences.

1. Borchers came to my office after receiving my letter in a hurry.
2. I told him for the last time I would pay his debts.
3. A business man does not have time to more than merely read the headlines.

CLEARNESS OF THOUGHT

4. We came into a cavern which is the home of bats, during certain portions of the year, innumerable.
5. He smiled when the servant brought the dessert and began to eat it greedily.
6. The young author read the review of the novel he had written for the seventh time.
7. I enjoyed the music as much as, if not more than, the sermon.
8. He waded through the water that rushed along in a pair of rubber boots.
9. The dentist gave a quick pull when I closed my eyes and extracted the tooth.
10. After adding up the totals, Farman complained about some of the expenditures, upon looking over his son's expense account.
11. He insisted for half an hour the object had not moved.
12. Hartwell showed me a letter, also borrowing the postage from me, that he intended to mail in answer to the advertisement.
13. The team should move as a unit, for one man going wrong will block the action or slow it down of the other ten.
14. If we can float the loan, we shall build the dam immediately, provided there are no legal complications.
15. Drama is a medium for ideas rather than for the portrayal of characters or action as written by Shaw.

PARALLEL STRUCTURE

When the structure of a sentence is simple and uniform, the important words strike the eye at once. Compare the following:

Parallel: Beggars must not be choosers.
Confusing: Beggars must not be the ones who choose.

A reader gives attention partly to the structure of a sentence, and partly to the thought. The less we puzzle him with our structure, the more we shall impress him with our thought.

Parallel: Seeing is believing. [Attention goes to the *thought*.]
Confusing: Seeing is to believe. [Attention is diverted to *structure*.]

The reader's expectation is that uniform structure shall accompany uniform ideas, and that a departure from uniformity shall indicate a change of thought.

Parallel Structure for Parallel Thoughts

30. Give parallel structure to those parts of a sentence which are parallel in thought. Do not needlessly interchange an infinitive with a participle, a phrase with a clause, a single word with a phrase or clause, a main clause with a dependent clause, one voice or mode of the verb with another, etc.

Faulty: Riding is sometimes better exercise than to walk.
Right: Riding is sometimes better exercise than walking. [Or]
    To ride is sometimes better exercise than to walk.
Faulty: He had two desires, of which the first was for money; in the second place, he wanted fame.

CLEARNESS BY PARALLEL STRUCTURE

Right: He had two desires, of which the first was for money and the second for fame. [Or] He had two desires: in the first place, he wanted money; in the second, fame.

Faulty: His rival handled cigars of better quality and having a higher selling price.

Right: His rival handled cigars of better quality and higher price.

Faulty: When you have mastered the operation of shifting gears, and after a little practice you will be a good driver.

Right: When you have mastered the operation of shifting gears, and had a little practice, you will be a good driver. [Or] After you master the gears and have a little practice, you will be a good driver.

Faulty: These are the duties of the president of a literary society:

    (a) To preside at regular meetings,
    (b) He calls special meetings,
    (c) Appointment of committees.

Right: These are the duties of the president of a literary society:

    (a) To preside at regular meetings,
    (b) To call special meetings,
    (c) To appoint committees.

Faulty: She was actively connected with the club, church, and with several organized charities. [Here parallelism is obscured by the omission from the second phrase of both the preposition and the article.]

Right: She was actively connected with the club, with the church, and with several organized charities.

Faulty: He was red-faced, awkward, and had a disposition to eat everything on the table. [The third element is like the others in thought, and should have similar form.]

Right: He had a red face, an awkward manner, and a disposition to eat everything on the table. [Or] He was red-faced, awkward, and voracious.

CLEARNESS BY PARALLEL STRUCTURE

Note.—Avoid misleading parallelism. For ideas *different* in kind, do *not* use parallel structure.

Wrong: He was hot, puffing, and evidently had run very hard. [The third element is unlike the others in thought; hence the *and* is misleading.]

Right: He was hot and puffing; evidently he had run very hard.

Confusing: He was admired for his knowledge of science, and for his taste for art, and for this I too honor him. [The last *for* gives a false parallelism to unlike thoughts.]

Better: He was admired for his scientific knowledge and for his artistic taste. I honor him for both these qualities.

Exercise:

1. The two ends of a hen's egg are unlike, but one end of the egg of a turtle is the same as the other.
2. The commonwealth was rent by two factions, of which one was republican; the wish of the other was that the monarchy should be restored.
3. The owner of the paper had a threefold aim: (1) unexcelled news service, (2) to furnish good editorial matter, (3) that his journal should be the favorite medium for advertisements.
4. The plumber was liked because of his skilful workmanship, and because of his friendly manner, and because of his steep bills we hated him.
5. The author opens the book by presenting the Dearborn girls, one called Laura, the other being named Page. Their parents having died, and since they are independent, the girls move to Chicago to live with an aunt.
6. Two common types are the spiral bandage and the figure eight, the former being used to wrap the limbs, and the latter is the manner the bandage is used in covering a joint.
7. In the classrooms the men learn reading and how to write, make hammocks, to repair shoes, do carpenter work, and a number of other useful things. Typewriting is also taught.

CLEARNESS BY PARALLEL STRUCTURE

Correlatives

Conjunctions that are used in pairs are called correlatives; for example, *not only . . but also . . , both . . and . . , either . . or . . , neither . . nor . . , not . . or . . , whether . . or . . .*

31. **Correlatives should usually be followed by elements parallel in form; if a predicate follows one, a predicate should follow the other; if a prepositional phrase follows one, a prepositional phrase should follow the other; and so on.**

Faulty: He was not only courteous to rich customers but also to poor ones. [Here the phrases intended to be balanced against each other are *to rich customers* and *to poor ones.* As the sentence stands, it is the word *courteous* that is balanced against *to poor ones.*]

Right: He was courteous not only to rich customers but also to poor ones.

Faulty: She could neither make up her mind to go nor could she decide to stay.

Right: She could neither make up her mind to go nor decide to stay. [Or] She could not make up her mind either to go or to stay.

Faulty: I talked both with Brown and Miller. [Here one conjunction is followed by a preposition and the other by a noun.]

Right: I talked with both Brown and Miller. [Or] I talked both with Brown and with Miller.

Exercise:

1. He could neither find that the trouble lay in the piston nor in the cylinder.
2. You can prepare your meals either in your own room or get them at a restaurant.

CLEARNESS BY CONSISTENCY

3. I lay listening to both the footsteps and my own heart beating.
4. The opossum was undecided whether to play dead or he thought it might be safer to dash for the tree.
5. The automobile has not only replaced the horse on the highways, but the tractor has replaced him in the fields.

CONSISTENCY

Shift in Subject or Voice

32. Do not needlessly shift the subject, voice, or mode in the middle of a sentence. Keep one point of view, until there is a reason for changing.

Faulty: In the stream which the road led over, fish were plentiful. [Here the first mental picture is of a stream. Then the thought is jerked away to the road above. Then it returns to the fish in the stream.]

Right: In the stream which flowed under the roadway, fish were plentiful.

Faulty: Mark Twain was born in the West, but the East was his home in later years. [The change of subject is uncalled for.]

Right: Mark Twain was born in the West, but lived in the East in his later years. [Or] The West was the birthplace of Mark Twain, and the East was his home in his later years.

Faulty: A careful driver can go fifteen miles on a gallon of gasoline, and at the same time very little lubricating oil is used. [The shift from active to passive voice is awkward and confusing.]

Right: A careful driver can go fifteen miles on a gallon of gasoline, and at the same time use very little lubricating oil.

Faulty: When a problem in chemistry is given, or when we wish to calculate certain formulas, we find that a knowledge of mathematics is indispensable.

CLEARNESS BY CONSISTENCY

Right: When a problem in chemistry is given, or when certain formulas are to be calculated, a knowledge of mathematics is indispensable. [Or] When we face a problem in chemistry, or wish to calculate certain formulas, we find that a knowledge of mathematics is indispensable.

Faulty: Next the ground should be harrowed. Then you sow the wheat. [The subject changes from *ground* to *you*. One verb explains what *should* be done, the other what somebody *does*.]

Right: Next the ground $\begin{Bmatrix} \text{is} \\ \text{should be} \end{Bmatrix}$ harrowed. Then it $\begin{Bmatrix} \text{is} \\ \text{should be} \end{Bmatrix}$ sown to wheat. [Or] Next you should harrow the ground. Then you should sow the wheat.

Exercise:
1. The cat played with the mouse, and tortured it, until it finally was killed.
2. Some of the girls are mindful of grandmother's counsel, and arctics are worn by them.
3. The paintings take him only a very short time to do, and he turns them out with very little effort.
4. By oiling and cleaning the machine you not only get better work out of it at the time, but also accumulations of dirt and grease will be prevented, which shorten its life.
5. Americans began work on the canal in 1906. The mistakes made by the French were of use to them. Congress voted to build a high-level lock system, and a sea-level route was considered too expensive.

Shift in Number, Person, or Tense

33. Avoid an inconsistent change in number, person, or tense.

Faulty change in number: One should save their money.
Right: People should save their money. [Or] A man should save his money.

CLEARNESS BY CONSISTENCY

Faulty change in person: Place the seeds in water, and in a few days a person can see that they have started to grow.

Right: Place the seeds in water, and in a few days you will see that they have started to grow.

Faulty change in number: Take your umbrella with you. They will be needed today.

Right: Take your umbrella with you. You will need it today.

Faulty change in tense: Freedom means that a man may conduct his affairs as he pleases so long as he did not injure anybody else.

Right: Freedom means that a man may conduct his affairs as he pleases so long as he does not injure anybody else.

Faulty change in tense: When he heard the news, he hurries down town and buys a paper.

Right: When he heard the news, he hurried down town and bought a paper.

Note.—A change of tense within a sentence is desirable and necessary in certain instances, for which see 55.

Sometimes, for the sake of vividness, past events are described in the present tense, as if they were taking place before our eyes. This usage is called the *historical present*. A shift to the historical present should not be made abruptly, or frequently, or for any subject except an important crisis.

Exercise:
1. At present every one is doing their best to prevent the spread of the disease.
2. If a person is careful about spending their pennies, your dollars will take care of themselves.
3. Potatoes should be so thoroughly cooked that there will not be a raw lump at the center of it.
4. To escape from the eyes of the world he goes to Sullivan's Island, where he lived with his servant, Jupiter.

5. Even a person working selfishly for their own interest **really** benefits the world, although he does not know it.

Mixed Constructions

34. Do not make a compromise between two constructions.

Faulty: I cannot help but go.
Right: I cannot help going. [Or] I cannot but go. [Or] I can but go.
Faulty: They are as following:
Right: They are as follows: [Or] They are the following:
Faulty: He tried, but of no avail.
Right: He tried, but to no avail. [Or] He tried, but his effort was of no avail.
Faulty: There is no honor to be on this committee.
Right: It is no honor to be on this committee. [Or] There is no honor in being on this committee.
Faulty: Sparks from the chimney caught the house on fire.
Right: Sparks from the chimney set the house on fire. [Or] The house caught fire from the sparks from the chimney.

Note.—The double negative and kindred expressions (*not hardly, not scarcely*, etc.) are an especially gross form of mixed construction.

Wrong: He isn't no better now than he was then. [Logically, *not no better* means *better*. The two negatives cancel each other and leave an affirmative.]
Right: He isn't any better now than he was then. [Or] He is no better now than he was then.
Wrong: She couldn't see her friend nowhere.
Right: She couldn't see her friend anywhere. [Or] She could see her friend nowhere.
Wrong: We couldn't hardly see through the mist.
Right: We could hardly see through the mist. [Or] We couldn't see well through the mist.

CLEARNESS BY CONSISTENCY

Exercise:
1. What difference does a few cents matter?
2. I see you have something on your mind which you want to tell it to me.
3. There is no advantage to rise too early.
4. I don't want to do this again never. In this wind one can't scarcely talk.
5. He was used to go around with a rough gang of fellows. He won't never forget your kindness.

Mixed Imagery

35. Avoid phrases which may call up conflicting mental images. When using metaphor, simile, etc., carry one figure of speech through, instead of shifting to another, or dropping suddenly back into literal speech.

Crude: The Republicans have gained a foothold in the heart of the cotton belt.
Right: The Republicans have gained a foothold in the South.
Crude: A key-note of sincerity should be the mainspring of a well-built speech. [*Key-note* suggests music; *mainspring* suggests mechanics; *well-built* suggests carpentry.]
Right: A key-note of sincerity should run through a good speech. [Or] Sincerity should be the mainspring and motive of a speech. [Or] Sincerity should be the foundation of a well-built speech.
Crude: He traveled a rough road and climbed with his burden the ladder of success, where he is a glowing example and guide to other men. [The suggestion which a reader with a sense of humor may get is, that a man starts out as a traveler, suddenly becomes a hod-carrier, and is then transformed into a bonfire or a lighthouse.]
Right: He traveled a rough road, but found success. Other men followed in his steps.

CLEARNESS BY CONNECTIVES

Incongruous: Spring came scattering flowers, and there was rain a great per cent of the time. [This sentence mingles the language of poetry with the language of science. It should be fanciful, or else literal, throughout.]

Right: Spring came scattering flowers and rain. [Or] Spring came with much rain and many flowers.

Exercise:

1. The strong arm of the law has taken a hand in the trouble.
2. This far-seeing insight enables him to cut the veil of time and to depict the future.
3. The room measured eleven feet by fourteen feet six inches, and was a veritable bower of beauty.
4. He shoveled some coal into the furnace, and then fired with a great purpose, began to solve problems in trigonometry.
5. The dawn stalked over the hills in her gray robes at 5:35.

USE OF CONNECTIVES

The Exact Connective

36. Use a connective which expresses the exact relation between two clauses. Distinguish between time and cause, concession and condition, etc. Do not overwork *and, so,* or *while*.

Misleading: *While* he is sick, he is able to walk. [Use *though*.]
Misleading: Miss Brown sang, *while* her sister spoke a piece. [Use *but*.]
Faulty: Work hard *when* you want to succeed. [Use *if*.]
Faulty: They will be sorry *without* they do this. [Use *unless*.]
Faulty: Little poetry is read, *only* at times when it is compulsory. [Use *except*.]
Faulty: The early morning and evening are the best times to find ducks, *and* we do not see many flying. [Use *and for that reason*.]

CLEARNESS BY CONNECTIVES

Faulty: Corbin says: "In America sportsmanship is almost a passion," *and* in England "the player very seldom forgets that he is a man first and an athlete afterward." [Use *whereas*.]

Note.—*So* is an elastic word that covers a multitude of vague meanings. Language has need of such a word, and in many instances (especially when the relation between clauses is obvious and does not need to be pointed out) *so* serves well enough. Use it, but not as a substitute for more exact connectives. Beware of falling into the *"so*-habit."

Abuse of *so* as a vague coördinating connective: So I went to call on Mrs. Woods, and so she told me about Mrs. White's new gown; so then I missed the car, and so of course our supper is late. [Strike out every *so*.]

Abuse of *so* as a subordinating connective: You may go, *so* you keep still. [Use *provided*.] *So* you do only that, I shall be satisfied. [Use *though*.]

Permissible: I was excited, so I missed the target.

So may be used, sparingly, to express result. But when a clause of result is important and needs emphasis, it is usually better to strike out *so* and subordinate the preceding clause.

Right: In my excitement I missed the target.
Right: Because I was excited, I missed the target.
Right: Being excited, I missed the target.

List of Connectives

A. With Coördinate Clauses, expressing

1. **Addition:** and, besides, furthermore, more than that, again, in addition, in like manner, likewise, moreover, then too, and what is more to the point, and what is even more interesting, and along with this, and finally.

CLEARNESS BY CONNECTIVES

2. **Contrast:** but, and yet, however, in spite of, in contrast to this, nevertheless, notwithstanding, nor, on the contrary, for all that, rather, still, but unhappily, yet unfortunately, whereas.
3. **Alternative:** or, nor, else, otherwise, neither, nor, or on the other hand.
4. **Consequence:** therefore, hence, consequently, accordingly, in this way, it follows that, the consequence is, and under such circumstances, and along with this, wherefore, thus, as a result, as a consequence.
5. **Explanation:** for example, for instance, in particular, more specifically, for, because.
6. **Repetition for emphasis:** in other words, that is to say, and assuredly, certainly, in fact, and in truth, indeed it is certain, undoubtedly, for example, in the same way, as I have said.

B. With Subordinate Adverb Clauses, expressing

1. **Time:** when, then, before, while, after, until at last, as long as, now that, upon which, until, until which event, whenever, whereupon, meanwhile.
2. **Place:** where, whence, whither, wherever.
3. **Degree or Comparison:** as, more than, rather than, than, to the degree in which.
4. **Manner:** as, as if, as though.
5. **Cause:** because, for, as, inasmuch. as, since, owing to the fact that, seeing that, in that.
6. **Purpose:** that, so that, in order that, lest.
7. **Result:** that is, so that, but that, whence it follows that, on account of which, because of which.
8. **Condition:** if, provided that, in case that, on condition that, supposing that, unless.
9. **Concession:** though, although, assuming that, admitting that, granting that, even if, no matter how, notwithstanding, of course, however much.

CLEARNESS BY CONNECTIVES

C. With Adjective Clauses. Adjective or relative clauses are introduced by who, which, that, or an equivalent compound.

Exercise:

Insert within the parentheses all connectives that might correctly be used, and underscore the one which you consider to be most exact:

1. Protestants were roasted, Jesuits hanged and quartered at Smithfield, and witches burned at Salem; (   ) these things were done by worthy people, who believed they had the best authority for their actions.
2. It is said that King George III winced when he first saw his homely little bride; (   ) he was a faithful husband.
3. Our host made a speech welcoming us in the most genial manner, (   ) we all felt at ease.
4. It is human nature to take delight in exciting admiration, (   ) children say "smart" things and "show off" when company is present.
5. Our representatives have promised to pass a new tax law in the next legislature; (   ) we must be patient.

Repetition of Connective with a Gain in Clearness

37. Connectives that accompany a parallel series should be repeated when clearness requires.

Preposition to be repeated: He was regarded as a hero by all who had known him at school, and especially his old school mates.

Right: He was regarded as a hero *by* all who had known him at school, and especially *by* his old school mates.

Sign of the infinitive to be repeated: He wishes to join with those who love freedom and justice, and end needless suffering.

Right: He wishes *to* join with those who love freedom and justice, and *to* end needless suffering.

CLEARNESS BY CONNECTIVES

Conjunction to be repeated: Since he was known to have succeeded in earlier enterprises, though confronted by difficulties that would have taxed the ability of older men, and his powers were now acknowledged to be mature, he was put in charge of the undertaking.

Right: *Since* he was known to have succeeded in earlier enterprises, though confronted by difficulties that would have taxed the ability of older men, and *since* his powers were now acknowledged to be mature, he was put in charge of the undertaking.

Conjunction to be repeated: He explained that the strikers asked only a fair hearing, since their contentions were misunderstood; were by no means in favor of the violent measures to which the public had grown accustomed; and had no desire to resort to bloodshed and the destruction of property.

Right: He explained *that* the strikers asked only a fair hearing, since their contentions were misunderstood; *that* they were by no means in favor of the violent measures to which the public had grown accustomed; and *that* they had no desire to resort to bloodshed and the destruction of property.

Exercise:

1. He likes sugar in his tea but not coffee.
2. From certain points he obtained beautiful views, especially the upper story of an old grist mill.
3. Joseph commanded their sacks to be filled with corn and money put back into the sacks.
4. Inasmuch as an obstruction now halted the automobile which had wildly run across the street and the traffic policeman took its number, I knew the guilty driver would be punished.
5. He told me that Lincoln had been born of poor parents, he had been reared in a log cabin, how as a boy he had studied under the greatest difficulties, and in a time of danger and trouble he had become president of the United States.

CLEARNESS BY CONNECTIVES

Repetition of Connective with a Loss in Clearness

38. Do not complicate thought by persistent repetition of elements beginning with *that, which, of, for,* or *but,* and NOT parallel in structure.

Complicated repetition of *that:* He gave a quarter to the boy that brought the paper that printed the news that the war was ended. [*That, which,* and *who* are often used carelessly to form a chain of subordinate clauses. Three sucessive subordinations are all that a reader can possibly keep straight; ordinarily a writer should not exceed two. But in parallel structure (See 30 and 37) the number of *that, which,* or *who* clauses does not matter; a writer may fill a page with them and not confuse the reader at all.]

Right: He gave the boy a quarter for bringing him the paper with the news that the war was ended.

Complicated repetition of *of:* The East Side Civics Club is an organization of helpers of the helpless of the lower classes of the city.

Right: The East Side Civics Club is organized to help the helpless poor of the city.

Complicated repetition of *for:* The general was dismayed, for he had not expected resistance, for he had thought the power of the enemy was shattered.

Right: The general was dismayed; he had not expected resistance, for he had thought the power of the enemy was shattered.

Complicated repetition of *but:* He was undoubtedly a brave man, but now he was somewhat alarmed, but he would not turn back.

Right: He was undoubtedly a brave man; though now somewhat alarmed, he would not turn back. [Or] He was undoubtedly a brave man. He was now somewhat alarmed, but he would not turn back.

CLEARNESS BY CONNECTIVES

Note.—Guard against the *but*-habit. Frequent recurrence of *but* makes the reader's thought "tack" or change its course too often. There are ways to avoid an excessive use of *but* and *however*. When one wishes to write about two things, A and B, which are opposed, he need not rush back and forth from one idea to the other. Let him first say all he wants to say about A. Then let him deliberately use the adversative *but,* and proceed to the discussion of B. In the following paragraph on "Whipping Children" the writer tries to be on both sides of the fence at once.

Confusing: It is easier to punish a child for a misdeed, than to explain and argue. *But* the gentler method is better. *Yet* we all admit that the birch must be used sometimes. *However,* if it is used only for serious transgressions, the child will have a sense of proportion regarding what offenses are grave. *But* for ordinary small misdemeanors I think we need a new motto: Spoil the rod and spare the child.

Right: It is easier to punish a child for a misdeed than to explain and argue. And of course we all admit that the birch must be used sometimes. *But* if it is used only for serious transgressions, the child will have a sense of proportion regarding what offenses are grave. For ordinary small misdemeanors I think we need a new motto: Spoil the rod and spare the child.

Exercise:

1. The cause of the explosion of the compound in the test-tube of the boy at the end of the table was not clear to the rest of us.
2. Gloucester, being of royal lineage, but having no authority, but being a shrewd man, decided he would rise in the world.
3. He had broken the lock which fastened the door that led into

CLEARNESS OF THOUGHT

the small room which they used instead of the living room, which was too hard to heat.
4. Then she decides to make peace with Eustacia, but when she is not admitted when she goes to the house, when she knows Eustacia and Clym are at home, then she goes away broken-hearted.
5. The officers make love to Marie, but she merely laughs them off. But there is one young Englishman who is more earnest than the rest. But he is very poor, although he is ambitious and energetic, too.

39. EXERCISE IN CLEARNESS OF THOUGHT

A. Parallel Structure

Give parallel structure to elements which are parallel in thought.

1. To send a full report by mail is better than if you dispatched a telegram.
2. He either must decide to vote with us or against us.
3. Hargreave asked for employment as manager, floor-walker, or even a book-keeping position.
4. We were delighted at the prospect of going up in an airship, and not pay a cent.
5. The only choice Evans had was either running the boat on the rocks, or to risk being swamped by the waves.
6. He was organizer, president, and had more of the stock than anybody else.
7. It was a matter of chagrin to both Republicans and to Democrats.
8. The tree on which the blossoms are shown first is the last one to bear the ripe fruit.
9. In his essay *Dream Children* Lamb discloses the fact that he led a lonely life, and his wish for a home of his own.
10. There are three ways to find out about the mind: introspection, by reading a text book, and to observe others.

CLEARNESS OF THOUGHT

11. First class passage is what people with plenty of money take. Poor people go by steerage.
12. They had to build their houses of logs, and build them not only for protection from the severe winters, but also from the Indians.
13. After you have turned on the water, and with a little adjustment of the nozzle, the hose throws a stream to the farthest corner of the yard.
14. The next step in the making of artificial flowers is that of giving hollow form to the petals, and the veins of the leaves are also made at the same time.
15. Forbes was not only faithful to his friends, but he was also unforgiving to his enemies.
16. Detroit is the center of the automobile-making industry. In Los Angeles most of our motion pictures are made.
17. Patrick Henry was considered one of America's best orators, he was a member of the Continental Congress, three times elected to the legislature, and governor of Virginia four times.
18. Soon this event was followed by the news of Heinrich's death, then his secretary was reported missing, and then, greatest shock of all, that Hugh had been killed.
19. Seventy-five years ago the demand for aluminum so far exceeded the supply that the cost was over fifty dollars a pound. You can buy a pound of aluminum now for a quarter because aluminum is so plentiful.
20. Egeria Park is bounded on the north and west by the Leighton Mesa on which we stand; in the southwest, the mighty Flat Tops rise like a wall several thousand feet into the air; on the south and southeast King Mountain lies, dark green with forests; while to the east the Black Tail Hills complete the circle and curve in to meet the mesa, being separated from it only by the channel of the Yampa River.

CLEARNESS OF THOUGHT

B. Shift in Subject or Voice

Rewrite the following sentences, avoiding unnecessary shift in construction.

1. The tigress paced back and forth in her cage, and everybody who came near was glared at by her.
2. The picture is then toned by dipping it into a solution of gold salts, or sometimes platinum salts may be used instead.
3. His hands were the hands of an artist. But a common laborer has feet like his.
4. Father picked up the *Times* and the important articles were read aloud by him.
5. Trunks carried as baggage should be well roped in order that you may not suffer through the rough handling they receive.
6. They began to quarrel violently, but it did not last long.
7. Williams' playing is brilliant and effective, yet he lacks the versatility of Tilden.
8. The credit is made up of the amounts in your favor. The amounts charged against you are called the debit.
9. When Wyatt developed his pictures, two exposures were found to have been made by him on one negative.
10. Macbeth paused, not knowing whether to kill Duncan, or whether he should be spared.
11. Finally, your hands should be buttered. You then take some candy and begin to pull it.
12. He did not lack courage; neither was industry wanting in him.
13. After the cat had played with the mouse for a while, it was eaten by her.
14. The broom is then inspected, and if found satisfactory, the cutting machine next trims it.
15. There are two kinds of destructive moths. We have long known the kind by which holes in cloth are eaten.

CLEARNESS OF THOUGHT

The other kind, which destroys trees, is a comparative newcomer among us.

C. Shift in Number, Person, or Tense

Rewrite the following sentences, removing all inconsistency in grammatical form.

1. When the directors heard of the investigation, they withhold the dividend.
2. Don't forget your ticket. They will be called for.
3. But one must learn to rise above worry, and bury your troubles.
4. Each of the students is given a chance to test their skill.
5. When windmills are motionless, the release of a wire will set it going.
6. He crawled from the wreckage and begins to berate the driver of the truck.
7. The Eskimo lives in the frozen latitudes, and their houses are built of ice.
8. Says he, "Is it cold?" "Not a bit," I replied, trying not to shiver.
9. When anybody borrows a pencil, you should not keep it the rest of your life.
10. Lilliput was a country in which a person is only six inches high, and their houses and live stock are in proportion.
11. If a person would sell when everybody was buying and buy when everybody is selling, they would make lots of money.
12. You will write letter after letter of application, and nobody answers you.
13. A person should not ride slower if the bicycle seems likely to fall, but go as fast as you can.
14. The manager stated they might use their leisure in any way they saw fit, provided they are on hand when work begins.

CLEARNESS OF THOUGHT

15. If a man hides in the underbrush and imitates the cry of a fledgling when it is seized, he would draw all the birds of the forest around him.

D. The Exact Connective

Insert within the parentheses all connectives which might correctly be used (See 36). Underscore the connective which you consider to be most exact:

1. I am afraid I cannot go, (   ) I should like to.
2. The cleverest tutors in the world could have done little to expand that small intellect, (   ) they might have improved his manners.
3. August came with all its sweltering heat, (   ) came harvest.
4. (   ) red lanterns had been left burning by the workmen, there was an accident.
5. The old society, with its courts and kings, fell to the ground, (   ) arose a new republic.
6. The quarterback should not have called for a forward pass; (   ) he should have signaled for a drop kick.
7. The explosions had become more regular, (   ) we thought the car would not give us any more trouble.
8. He would not betray me; (   ) he would understand and help me.
9. Only during the hops season are these beggars able to make even a little money. (   ) they are sent to the workhouse.
10. She wore a picture hat, (   ) turbans were then the style.
11. He did not know how to row; (   ) he took one of the oars and used it as a paddle.
12. Necessity knows no law; (   ) you cannot much blame Jean Valjean for stealing a loaf of bread.
13. Let us say that Cooper's syntax is now and then at fault, and that he commits a few technical errors; shall

CLEARNESS OF THOUGHT

we (   ) condemn an entire book which tells a lively story?

E. Subordinating Connectives

Each of the following sentences contains an idea which is, or may be, subordinate to another idea. (1) Decide what kind of subordinate relation should exist between the ideas. (2) Determine what connective best expresses this relation. (Consult 36 for a list of connectives.) (3) Write the sentence as it should be.

1. No one can get into the civil service without he passes an examination.
2. He caught a string of fish about noon, when they bite best in early morning or late evening.
3. While I was eating my dinner, I was not really hungry in the least.
4. He stubbornly refused to shift to a lower gear, and the car failed to climb the hill.
5. The bomb fell amid a group of soldiers when one of them seized it and threw it out of the trench.
6. The door blew shut so hard, and the vase fell from the mantel.
7. Since I came to live in this village, you ought to infer that I do not dislike it.
8. He never did his best only when circumstances forced him to.
9. Cook had lived by the sea all his life, and he couldn't swim.
10. I shall be glad to call Thursday, just so it is convenient for you.
11. Stay away from the oil stock promoters when you don't want to lose all your money.
12. It was a shady spot, so we spread out our lunch. We began to eat, and a bull appeared, and so we left in a hurry.

CLEARNESS OF THOUGHT

F. Repetition of Connectives

In the following sentences determine whether repetition is desirable or undesirable, and change the sentences accordingly.

1. We were fortunate to be able to begin to work today.
2. Basketball is a game that I played during all the years that I was in that school.
3. It was through character that he had won their support, and in particular courtesy.
4. He said that a roast will be well done that is left a few hours in a fireless cooker that holds the heat like the one that his company manufactures.
5. They saw that the entire roof had been blown loose and hung over the street and the chimney was rocking dangerously.
6. The bill which now lies before us has aroused great opposition, of which the strongest comes from the faction which I represent.
7. With this remark, in walked an old man with a dog with a stumpy tail.
8. Our guide was familiar with palaces where princes had lived in luxury and pride, and also tombs.
9. It was a bad plan, but very popular with the taxpayers, but opposed by the mayor, city attorney, and by two aldermen.
10. The lieutenant ordered us to dig a trench which would carry away the surface water and not touch the canvas overhead, so that the tent would be dry.
11. So then I was made chairman of the Committee on Home Improvement, so of course I had no time to do housework, so I just had to have a servant.
12. Nothing pleased him more than to dress up in brother's band uniform, get him an old broom for a gun, stand erect at the head of his imaginary regiment and give commands: "Forward, march!"

CLEARNESS OF THOUGHT

13. He was ambitious, but he was inexperienced. But he could learn rapidly, and gave promise of becoming a good executive. Still, their immediate need was for a competent manager for the export department. Nevertheless, the wisest plan might be to employ a young man and train him for the position. However, what they finally told him was that they hoped he would keep in touch with them.

EMPHASIS

Emphasis by Position

40. Reserve the emphatic positions in a sentence for important words or ideas. (The emphatic positions are the beginning and the end — especially the end.)

Weak ending: Then like a flash a vivid memory of my uncle's death came to me.
Weak: I demand the release of the prisoners, in the first place.
Weak: This principle is one we cannot afford to accept, if my understanding of the question is correct.

Place the important idea at the end. Secure, if possible, an emphatic beginning. "Tuck in" unimportant modifiers.

Emphatic: Like a flash came to me a vivid memory of my uncle's death.
Emphatic: I demand, in the first place, the release of the prisoners.
Emphatic: This principle, if my understanding of the question is correct, is one we cannot afford to accept.

Exercise:
1. The game was full of thrills, from start to finish, in both attack and defence.
2. The man is a coward who will not back such a cause, disregarding party politics.
3. Markheim had committed murder, and was now battling with gruesome visions in that solitary place.
4. These men knew that, alive or dead, their names would live forever on the lips of the people, when they went into the battle.
5. You are much at fault, if I may venture to say so. His conduct, also, is simply atrocious, to my way of thinking. All of us have faults, it seems.

Emphasis by Separation

41. An idea which needs much emphasis should be detached, and allowed to stand in a sentence by itself. (See 10.)

Faulty: The flames were by this time beyond control, and the walls collapsed, and several firemen were hurt. [The ideas here are too important to be run together in one sentence.]

Right: By this time the flames were beyond control, and the walls collapsed. Several firemen were hurt.

A quotation gains emphasis when it is separated from what follows.

Weak: "The best laid schemes o' mice an' men
                Gang aft a-gley,"
are some lines from Burns which McDonald was always quoting.

Emphatic: "The best laid schemes o' mice an' men
                Gang aft a-gley."
McDonald was always quoting these lines from Burns.

Direct discourse is more emphatic when it is separated from explanatory phrases, particularly from those which follow.

Weak: Mosher leaped to the stage and shouted defiantly, "I will never consent to that!" and he looked as if he meant what he said.

Right: Mosher leaped to the stage and shouted his defiance. "I will never agree to that!" And he looked as if he meant what he said.

Exercise:

1. Mr. Randolph was born in Centerville and lived in Ohio where my father knew him well, and last night he had a bad accident.
2. The ice piled up and formed a great bridge below the falls;

EMPHASIS BY SUBORDINATION

so solid was this bridge that it did not melt for weeks, and people came for miles to see it.

3. The doctor shook his head and said, "Adenoids," and I felt foolish at having supposed the tonsils could be in such a place.
4. Then I heard a voice out of the dark, above the roar of the wind, "Get a line to us; the boat's filling fast;" and immediately the docks were in confusion.
5. Certain lines from a pirate song in one of Stevenson's books,
    "Fifteen men on the dead man's chest—
    Yo-ho-ho, and a bottle of rum!"
    have stuck in my memory since childhood.

Emphasis by Subordination

Do not place the important idea of a sentence in a subordinate clause or phrase. Make the important idea grammatically independent. If possible, subordinate the rest of the sentence to it. (See 15.)

Faulty: He had a manner which made me angry.
Faulty: The fire spread to the third story, when the house was doomed.
Faulty: For years the Indians molested the white people, thereby causing the settlers to want revenge.

The important idea should not be placed in a *which* clause, or a *when* clause, or a participial phrase.

Right: His manner made me angry.
Right: When the fire spread to the third story, the house was doomed.
Right: Years of molestation by the Indians made the white men want revenge.

Exercise:
1. His exhibit was the best, taking the prize.
2. I sat there quietly reading, when there was an explosion.

EMPHASIS BY PERIODIC STRUCTURE

3. In high mountains the intense light beats down on the snow, which blinds the eyes.
4. I was about to fall asleep, when I realized that some one was looking at me.
5. He asked me to press a small lever on the side of the machine, which I did.

The Periodic Sentence

A sentence is periodic when the completion of the main thought is delayed until the end. This delay creates a feeling of suspense. A periodic sentence is doubly emphatic: it has emphasis by position because the important idea comes at the end; it has emphasis by subordination because all ideas except the last one are grammatically dependent.

43. To give emphasis to a loosely constructed sentence, turn it into periodic form.

Loose: I saw two men fight a duel, many years ago, on a moonlit summer night, in a little village in northern France. [What is most important, the time? the place? or the actual duel? Place the important idea last.]

Periodic: Many years ago, on a moonlit summer night, in a little village in northern France, I saw two men fight a duel.

Loose: We left Yellowstone Gateway for the ride of our lives in a six-horse tally-ho. [Place the important idea last, *and make all other ideas grammatically subordinate.*]

Periodic: Leaving Yellowstone Gateway in a six-horse tally-ho, we had the ride of our lives.

Loose: The river was swollen with incessant rain, and it swept away the dam. [Which is the important idea? Why not make it appear more important by subordinating everything to it?]

EMPHASIS BY CLIMAX

Periodic: The river, swollen with incessant rain, swept away the dam.

Loose: War means to have our pursuit of knowledge and happiness rudely broken off, to feel the sting of death and bereavement, to saddle future generations with a burden of debt and national hatred.

Periodic: To have our pursuit of knowledge and happiness rudely broken off, to feel the sting of death and bereavement, to saddle future generations with a burden of debt and national hatred—this is war.

Exercise:

1. The wild fox dug his hole unscared, on the spot where you now stand, four-score years ago.
2. There is a little one-room cabin tucked away in a "draw" of the North Dakota Bad Lands, forty miles from a railroad.
3. The directors signed the contract, greatly to my surprise, in spite of the delay, and to the consternation of all my relatives.
4. Peter the Great, in 1697, decided to make a tour of western Europe, having conquered the Turks and the Tartars, and having his own dominions well in hand.
5. The chapel of William Tell stands by the soft, blue waters of Lake Lucerne. On the anniversary of his revolt and victory, the light boats of the allied cantons skim across those waters, as they glitter in the July sun.

Order of Climax

1. In a series of words, phrases, or clauses of noticeable difference in strength, use the order of climax.

Wrong order: He was insolent and lazy.

Weak ending: Literature has expanded into a sea, where before it was only a small stream.

Weak ending: As we listened to his story we felt the sordid misery and the peril and fear of war.

EMPHASIS BY BALANCED STRUCTURE

Emphatic: He was lazy and insolent.
Emphatic: The stream of literature has swollen into a torrent, expanded into a sea.
Emphatic: As we listened to his story we felt the fear, the peril, the sordid misery of war.

Exercise:

1. Hawkins was convulsed, Southby amused.
2. The story printed there is a wretched lie, entirely false.
3. Gower put into his pocket five hundred dollars, a handkerchief, and a cigarette case.
4. He gave a terrible cry in his desperation, in his alarm, in his surprise.
5. The telephone has rescued the farmer from isolation, and freed the city dweller from petty inconveniences.

The Balanced Sentence

45. Two ideas similar or opposite in thought gain in emphasis when set off, one against the other, in similar constructions.

Weak and straggling: This paper, like many others, has many bad features, but in some ways it is very good. The news articles are far better than the editorials, which are feeble.
Balanced structure: This paper is in some respects good; in other respects very poor. The news articles are impressive; the editorials are feeble.
Weak and complicated: From the East a man who lives in the West can learn a great deal, and an Easterner ought to be able to understand the West.
Balanced: A Westerner can learn much from the East, and an Easterner needs to understand the West.
Weak: Both Mill and Macaulay influenced the younger writers. Mill taught some of them to reason, but many more of them learned from Macaulay only a superficial eloquence.

EMPHASIS BY THE ACTIVE VOICE

Balanced: Both Mill and Macaulay influenced the younger writers. If Mill taught some of them to reason, Macaulay tempted many more of them to declaim.

Note.—Although excessive use of balance is artificial, occasional use of it is powerful. It can give to writing either dignity (as in an oration) or point (as in an epigram). Observe how many proverbs are in balanced structure. "Seeing is believing.—Nothing venture, nothing have.—For every grain of wit there is a grain of folly.—You cannot do wrong without suffering wrong.—An eye for an eye, a tooth for a tooth." Note the effective use of balance in Emerson's *Essays*, particularly in *Compensation;* and in the Old Testament, particularly in *Psalms* and *Proverbs*.

Exercise:

1. A foreigner spends money less recklessly than an American, who is usually extravagant.
2. He worked very hard to make himself efficient, and also with the idea of attaining the good will of his employer.
3. With cold water you can remove grease from a cloth, but the result will be different if hot water is used.
4. Instead of equipping a student for work in the world, he often leaves college with a mixture of dead languages and live nonsense.
5. By walking too fast for the first half hour a person wears himself out at once. But he can go till nightfall if he begins moderately.

The Weak Effect of the Passive Voice

6. Use the active voice unless there is a reason for doing otherwise. The passive voice is, as the name implies, not emphatic.

EMPHASIS BY REPETITION

Weak: Your gift is appreciated by me.
Better: I appreciate your gift.
Weak and vague: His step on the porch was heard.
Better: His step sounded on the porch. [Or] I heard his step on the porch.

The passive voice is especially objectionable when by failing to indicate the agent of the verb it unnecessarily mystifies the reader.

Vague: The train was seen speeding toward us.
Better: We saw the train speeding toward us.

Exercise:
1. After a hearty supper had been eaten, Robert went to bed.
2. Woolen stockings are comfortable because the moisture of the feet is absorbed by them.
3. A great deal of fun was had by the few who were able to be on deck.
4. Wednesday being a day on which we had no classes was decided to be the best day.
5. At the age of twenty-one Bennett left his home town and went to London, where great ability as an artist was soon shown by him. After ten years the greatest success was achieved.

Effective Repetition

47a. The simplest and most natural way to emphasize a word or an idea is to repeat it. The Bible is the best standard of simplicity and dignity in our language, and the Bible uses repetition constantly. A word or idea that is repeated must, of course, be important enough to deserve emphasis.

Fairly emphatic: He works and toils and labors, but he seems never to get anywhere.

EMPHASIS BY REPETITION

Very emphatic: Work, work, work, all he does is work, and still he seems never to get anywhere.

Fairly emphatic: How did the general meet this new menace? He withdrew before it!

Very emphatic: How did the general meet this new menace? He withdrew! He retreated! He ran away!

Homely but emphatic: "I went under," said the old salt; "bows. gunnels, and starn—all under."

Deliberately too emphatic: Everywhere we hear of efficiency—efficiency experts, efficiency bureaus, efficiency methods, in the office, in the school, in the home—until one longs to fly to some savage island beyond the reach of inhuman modern science.

0. Not only words, but an entire grammatical structure may be repeated on a large scale for emphasis.

Weak: We hope that this shipment will reach you in good condition, and that you will favor us with other orders in the future, which will be given prompt and courteous attention. [This sentence is flimsy and spineless because the writer had a timid reluctance to repeat.]

Strong: We hope that this shipment will reach you in good condition. We believe that the quality of our goods will induce you to send us a second order. We assure you that such an order will receive prompt and courteous attention. [Note the emphasis derived from the resolute march of the expressions *We hope, We believe, We assure*.]

Emphatic: After years of fruitless labor he could but feel bitter disappointment—disappointment that men were so selfish, disappointment that he himself had not always been true to his ideals.

Emphatic: Thus died the peasant girl that had delivered France; died thinking of her home in Domremy, died amidst the tears of ten thousand enemies, died amidst the drums and trumpets of armies.

Emphatic and natural: This corner of the garden was my

EMPHASIS BY VARIETY

first playground. Here I made my first toddling effort to walk. Here on the soft grass I learned the delight of out-of-doors. Here I became acquainted with the bull-frog, and the bumble-bee, and the neighbor's dog.

Emphatic and delightful: He maketh me to lie down in green pastures; he leadeth me beside the still waters. He restoreth my soul; he leadeth me in the paths of righteousness for his name's sake.

Exercise:

1. It rains. Continually I hear the water dripping.
2. The convict kept waiting for a pardon.
3. Boland, having asked for a dime's worth, came back from the Filipino's stall with bananas in his clothes everywhere.
4. The battle began. Fired by their leader's words, the Greeks struck their mightiest blows, struck for their homes and their native land, justice and freedom.
5. The plowman was weary from the long hours, the heat, and dust. For a very long time he plodded, turning the furrows across the field.

Offensive Repetition

Careless repetition attracts attention to words that do not need emphasis. It is extremely annoying to the reader.

48a. Unless a word or phrase is repeated deliberately to gain force or clearness, its repetition is a blunder. Get rid of recurring expressions in one of three ways: (1) by substituting equivalent expressions, (2) by using pronouns more liberally, (3) by rearranging the sentence so as to say once what has awkwardly been said twice. Each of these schemes is illustrated below.

EMPHASIS BY VARIETY

1. Repetition cured by the use of equivalent expressions (synonyms).

   Bad: *Just* as we were half way down the lake, *just* off Milwaukee, we *began* to feel a slight motion of the ship and the *wind began* to freshen. The *wind began* to blow more fiercely from the south and the waves *began* to leap high. The boat *began* to pitch and roll.

   Right: *Just* as we were half way down the lake, *opposite* Milwaukee, we began to feel a slight motion of the ship, for the wind *had* freshened. Before long *a gale, blowing* from the south, *kicked up a heavy sea and caused* the boat to pitch and roll. [Notice how combining the last two sentences helps to solve the problem of the last *began,* besides giving firmer texture to the construction.]

2. Repetition cured by the use of pronouns. (In using this method, one should take care that the reference of the pronouns is clear.)

   Bad: The *Law Building,* the *Commerce Building,* and the *Science Building* are close together. The *Commerce Building* is south of the *Law Building,* and the *Science Building* is south of the *Commerce Building.* The *Law Building* is old and dilapidated. The *Commerce Building* is a red brick *building,* trimmed in terra-cotta. The *Science Building* resembles the *Commerce Building.*

   Right: The Law, Commerce, and Science Buildings are close together in a row. *The first of these* is old and dilapidated. South of *it* stands the Commerce Building, *which,* because of *its* red brick and terra-cotta trimmings, somewhat resembles the Science Building.

3. Repetition cured by rearranging and condensing.

   Bad: The *autumn* is my favorite of all the *seasons.* While *autumn* in the *city* is not such a pleasant *season* as *autumn*

EMPHASIS BY VARIETY

in the country, yet even in the *city* my preference will always be for the *autumn*.

Right: My favorite season is autumn. I like it best in the country, but even in the city it is the best time of the year.

b. Avoid a monotonous repetition of sentence structure. To give variety to successive sentences: (1) vary the length, (2) vary the beginnings, (3) avoid a series of similar compound sentences, (4) interchange loose with periodic structure, (5) use rhetorical question, exclamation, direct discourse, (6) avoid an excessive use of participles or adjectives.

1. Vary the length of sentences.

    Bad: Walter came up the path carrying Betty in his arms. She was wet from head to toe. Damp curls clung to her pale face. Water dripped from her clothes. One hand hung loosely over Walter's arm. The other held a live duckling. She had saved the little duck from drowning. This was Betty's first day in the country.

    Right: Walter came up the path carrying Betty in his arms— little Betty who was spending her first day in the country. She was wet from head to toe; damp curls clung to her pale face, and water dripped from her clothes. In one hand she held a live duckling. Her face lighted with courage as she told how she jumped into the pond and saved the little duck from drowning.

2. Vary the beginnings of sentences. Do not allow too many sentences to begin with the subject, or with a time clause, or with a participle, or with *so*. When you have finished a composition, rapidly read over the opening words of each sentence, to see if there is sufficient variety.

EMPHASIS BY VARIETY

Bad [too many sentences begin directly with the subject]: Our way is circuitous. A sharp turn brings us round a rocky point. The road drops suddenly into a little valley. The roof of a house appears in a grove of trees below. A cottage is there and a flower garden. An old-fashioned well is near the door.

Right: Presently, on our circuitous way, we make a sharp turn round a rocky point. Before us the road drops suddenly into a little valley. In a grove of trees below appears the roof of a house, and as we draw nearer we see a cottage surrounded by flowers. Nothing could be more attractive to a weary traveler than the old-fashioned well near the door.

3. Avoid a series of similar compound sentences, especially those of two parts of equal length, joined by *and* or *but*.

Bad: Ring was a sheep dog, and tended the flock with his master. One day there came a deep snow, and the flock did not return. They found the herder frozen stiff, and the dog shivering beside him.

Right: Ring was a sheep dog, and tended the flock with his master. One day there came a deep snow. When the flock failed to return, the men became uneasy, and began a search. They found the herder frozen stiff, with the dog shivering beside him.

4. Change occasionally from loose to periodic or balanced structure (See 43 and 45).

Monotonous: I stood at the foot of Tunbridge hill. I saw on the horizon a dense wood, which, in the evening sunlight, was veiled in purple haze [Loose]. On the left was the village, the houses appearing like specks in the distance [Loose]. Nearer on the right was the creek, winding through the willows [Loose]. The creek approached nearer until it reached the dam, over which it rushed tumultuously [Loose]. Near by was a thicket of tall trees, through which I could see the

EMPHASIS BY VARIETY

white tents of my fellow campers, and their glowing camp fires [Loose].

Right: Far south from Tunbridge hill, on the dim horizon, I saw, veiled in the evening haze, a dense wood [Periodic, long, conveying the idea of distance better than a loose sentence]. On my left stood the village, the houses like specks; on my right wound the creek, nearer and nearer through the willows [Balanced]. The creek advanced by slow sinuous turns, until, reaching the dam, it plunged over tumultuously [Loose]. Through a thicket of tall trees, near at hand, I could see the white tents of my fellow campers, and their glowing camp fires [Periodic through the middle of the sentence; then loose].

5. Use question, exclamation, direct quotation.

Somewhat flat: He asked me the road to Camden. I did not know. I told him to ask Thurber, who knew the country well.
Better: He asked me the road to Camden. The road to Camden? How should I know? "Ask Thurber," I said impatiently; "he knows this country. I'm a stranger."

6. Avoid an excessive use of participles. Do not pile adjectives around every noun. Above all, do not form a habit of using adjectives in pairs or triplets.

Bad: Sitting by the window, I saw a sharp, dazzling flash of lightning, and heard a loud rumbling crash of heavy thunder, warning me of the coming of the storm. Darting across the gray, leaden sky, the quick, jagged lightning flashed incessantly. The tall stately poplar trees thrashed around in the boisterous wind. Then across the window, like a great white curtain, swept the streaming, blinding rain.
Right: I sat by the window. Suddenly a sharp flash of lightning and a roll of thunder gave warning of the approach of a storm. Soon lightning zig-zagged across the sky incessantly. The wind thrashed the poplar trees. Then like a white curtain across the window streamed the rain.

EMPHASIS

Exercise:
1. It is a banquet which is given annually. The toasts which are given at this banquet are usually given by seniors.
2. In sealing a package with sealing-wax you must first moisten the seal or the hot sealing-wax will stick to it.
3. He could not work the mine alone, so he went to Winnemucca and brought back with him six miners. When the miners arrived, they began to work the mine with great speed.
4. The duck at the apex of the wedge has to overcome the full resistance of the atmosphere as no other duck does, and when this leading duck drops back exhausted, another duck takes its place.
5. Being in the infantry, he wanted to become a good infantryman. Having a copy of the Infantry Drill Regulations, he studied it faithfully. Knowing some of the more seasoned infantrymen, he asked them questions.

49. EXERCISE IN EMPHASIS

A. Lack of Emphasis in General

Make the following sentences emphatic.

1. "Your mother is dying," the doctor said.
2. The bank is in a bad way, according to reports.
3. The hare found the tortoise there before him, much to his chagrin.
4. One hundred thousand large business concerns fail every year, the speaker said.
5. The stable boy ran a nail in his foot and contracted lockjaw, death being the result.
6. "Lycidas" is the most important poem in the *Golden Treasury*, as it seems to me.
7. The wolf said, "If you don't open the door, I'll give a huff and a puff and blow your house in," but the little pig wouldn't.

EMPHASIS

8. Upon my attorney's advice I refused to say anything when questioned about the matter.
9. The man is not a true athletic director who neglects the training of the majority of the students.
10. Gladstone chewed every bite of his food thirty-two times, once for each tooth, as you may have heard.
11. Dutch art dropped dead at the end of the seventeenth century, as I have remarked before.
12. Of course I went flying over the horse's head, but fortunately landed in a shrub which broke my fall, and I was little worse for my experience except for a cut lip.

B. Loose or Unemphatic Structure

Make the following sentences more emphatic by throwing them into periodic form.

1. They fought their way into the citadel, little by little, an inch at a time.
2. Norman struck the last match, while the rest of us bent forward with sheltering hands.
3. I had been in the wrong, as I perceived afterward.
4. Bob made a wild dash, thinking the train was pulling out.
5. Use a vacuum cleaner if you want to keep your rugs from getting filled with dust.
6. They struggled on under the scorching sun, in choking dust, across the desert, from daylight to dark.
7. You should join a building association if you lack ready money to build a house.
8. The coffee-pot toppled over when the stick burned through, just as Kirby predicted.
9. On yellowish cigarettes he was forever smoking, or on cheap, ragged-looking cigars, or on smelly cob pipes.
10. Leeds crossed the line first, having cleared the last hurdle a fraction of a second ahead of Bonner.

EMPHASIS

11. He defaulted after keeping every promise all these years, redeeming every obligation, and winning every man's regard.
12. She had her reward in the happy faces of the children and in the silence that meant more than words.
13. The stream pushed its way to the sea down rocky defiles, across broad, verdant meadows, and through the shadowed quiet of forests.

C. Faulty Repetition

Repetition in the following sentences is objectionable, because it attracts attention to words or constructions that do not need to be emphasized. Improve the sentences, avoiding unnecessary repetition.

1. I took a long look at the car that took me over that perilous road.
2. Upon inquiry I was told they had a room, and I felt much relieved to have found a room.
3. We were finding good ore, and found we had almost enough to make a shipment to the mill.
4. My first expense is for house rent and food. House rent and food take half of my income.
5. He stood on a downtown corner and watched the stream of traffic roll down both sides of the street.
6. I said I would pick the duck. But when I got to picking it, I found that a duck is about the hardest bird on earth to pick. I determined to pick an easier task next time.
7. The old course of the river was a horseshoe-shaped course, whereas the new course cut straight across. Also, the new course was a mile shorter than the old course.
8. The tornado now increased in violence. It caught a tree and tore it from its roots. It ripped the roof from the barn and threw it over into the pasture. It turned a wagon over on its side. Then it seemed to lose its fury.

EMPHASIS

9. The skilled laborer may be in reality an unskilled laborer who gets money under false pretenses by exchanging labor that is unskilled for pay due skilled labor only.
10. To find a bee-tree, you catch a bee in one part of the field, release him, and watch which way he flies; then do the same by another bee in another part of the field; and finally find the bee-tree by finding where the bee-lines intersect.

GRAMMAR

Case

50a. The subject of a verb is in the nominative case, even when the verb is remote, or understood (not expressed).

Wrong: They are as old as us.
Right: They are as old as we [are].
Wrong: He is taller than her.
Right: He is taller than she [is].

Note.—*Than* and *as* are conjunctions, not prepositions. When they are followed by a pronoun merely, this pronoun is not their object, but part of a clause the rest of which may be understood. The case of this pronoun is determined by its relation to the rest of the unexpressed clause. Sometimes the understood clause calls for the objective: "I like his brother better than [I like] him." *Than whom*, though ungrammatical, is sanctioned by usage.

b. Guard against the improper attraction of *who* into the objective case by intervening expressions like *he says*.

Wrong: The man whom they believed was the cause of the trouble left the country. [*They believed* is parenthetical, and the subject of *was* is *who*.]
Right: The man who they believed was the cause of the trouble left the country.
Wrong: Whom do you suppose made us a visit?
Right: Who do you suppose made us a visit?

GRAMMAR—CASE

Guard against the improper attraction of *who* or *whoever* into the objective case by a preceding verb or preposition.

> Wrong: Punish whomever is guilty. [The pronoun is the subject of *is*. The object of *punish* is the entire clause *whoever is guilty.*]
> Right: Punish whoever is guilty.
> Wrong: The mystery as to whom had rendered him this service remained. [The pronoun is the subject of *had rendered*. The object of the preposition is the entire clause *who had rendered him this service.*]
> Right: The mystery as to who had rendered him this service remained.

c. Nouns or pronouns connected by the verb *to be* (in any of its forms, *is, was, were, be,* etc.) agree in case. *To be* never takes an object, because it does not express action.

> Wrong: Was it her? Was it them? It is me.
> Right: Was it she? Was it they? It is I.
> Wrong: The happiest people there were him and his mother.
> Right: The happiest people there were he and his mother.
> Wrong: They declared the culprit to be he and no other.
> Right: They declared the culprit to be him and no other.

d. The object of a preposition or a verb is in the objective case.

> Wrong: Some of we fellows went fishing.
> Right: Some of us fellows went fishing.
> Wrong: That seems incredible to you and I.
> Right: That seems incredible to you and me.
> Wrong: Who did they detect?
> Right: Whom did they detect?

GRAMMAR—CASE

e. The "assumed" subject of an infinitive is in the objective case.

Right: I wanted him to go. [*Him to go* is the group object of the verb *wanted*. *To go*, being an infinitive, cannot assert an action, and consequently cannot take a subject. But *to go* implies that something is at least capable of going. *Him* is the logical, or latent, or assumed subject of *to go*.]

Right: *Whom* do you wish *to be* your leader? [*Whom* is the assumed subject of the infinitive *to be*.]

f. A noun or pronoun used to express possession is in the possessive case. Do not omit the apostrophe (See 97) from nouns, or from the pronouns *one's* and *other's*. Most of the other possessive pronouns do not require an apostrophe.

Right: The man's hair is gray.
Right: The machine does its work well. [*It's* would mean *it is*.]
Right: One should do one's duty.

g. A noun or pronoun linked with a gerund should be in the possessive case whenever the use of the objective case might cause confusion.

Faulty: Is there any criticism of Arthur going?
Right: Is there any criticism of Arthur's going?
Right: I had not heard of his being sick.
Right, but slightly less desirable: I had not heard of him being sick.

Note.—In other instances than those in which clearness is involved many good writers use the objective case with the gerund. But even in these instances most writers prefer the possessive case.

GRAMMAR—CASE

h. It is usually awkward and slightly illogical to attribute possession to inanimate objects.

Awkward: The farm's management.
Better: The management of the farm.
Awkward: The stomach's lining.
Better: The lining of the stomach.

Note.—Usage justifies many exceptions, particularly (1) expressions that involve time or measure, *a day's work, a hair's breadth, a year's salary, a week's vacation, a cable's length;* and (2) expressions that involve personification, explicit or implied, *Reason's voice, the law's delay, for mercy's sake, the heart's desire, the tempest's breath.*

i. A pronoun agrees with its antecedent in person, gender, and number, but not in case.

Right: *I, who am* older, know better.
Right: Tell *me, who am* older, your trouble.
Right: Many a man has saved *himself* by counsel.

Exercise:

1. You are an inch taller than —— [I, me]. The players on the other team weigh more than —— [we, us]. We are not so awkward as —— [they, them].
2. Is that —— [he, him]? It was —— [she, her]. The luckiest men in the mining camp will be —— [he, him] and his partner. It is —— [I, me].
3. Three of —— [we, us] fellows have a room on the second floor. To —— [he, him] and —— [I, me] a suggestion of that kind makes no appeal. In a far corner sat two men —— [who, whom] I decided were bachelors.
4. —— [Ones, One's] relatives may be the chief reason for —— [one, one's] staying at home. My parents had high hopes

GRAMMAR—NUMBER

of —— [my, me] going to college. —— [Who, Whom] would you like to go riding with us?

5. —— [Who, Whom] do you think called me just now? The man —— [who, whom] Parlin says was his chauffeur runs a real estate office. I was surprised to hear of —— [his, him] becoming rich. The uncertainty as to —— [who, whom] owns the land has been ended.

Number

51a. *Each, every, every one, everybody, anybody, either, neither, no one, nobody,* and similar words are singular.

Wrong: Everybody did their best.
Right: Everybody did his best.
Wrong: Each of my three friends were there.
Right: Each of my three friends was there.
Wrong: Either of the candidates are capable of making a good officer.
Right: Either of the candidates is capable of making a good officer.

b. Do not let *this* or *that* when modifying *kind* or *sort* be attracted into the plural by a following noun.

Wrong: He knew nothing of those kind of activities.
Right: He knew nothing of that kind of activities.
Wrong: I never did like these sort of post cards.
Right: I never did like this sort of post cards.

c. Collective nouns may be regarded as **singular or plural**, according to the meaning intended.

Right: The crowd is waiting.
Right: The crowd are not agreed.

GRAMMAR—AGREEMENT

Right: Webster maintained that the United States is an inseparable union; Hayne that the United States are a separable union.

English usage: The government were considering a new bill regarding labor.

American usage: The government was glad to place our troops at the disposal of General Foch.

d. Do not use *don't* in the third person singular. Use *doesn't*. *Don't* is a contraction of *do not*.

Wrong: He don't get up early on Sunday morning.
Right: He doesn't get up early on Sunday morning.

Exercise:

1. He don't like those kind of gloves. The waiter is more polite to these kind of people.
2. Each of us wore a very sad look on our face. Evidently neither of these reasons are true reasons.
3. Every dog has their day. After the long trip nobody was looking their best. Is there any of us who have not suffered from a sense of dishonesty?
4. She don't have many letters to write until late in the morning. It don't seem as if we should. He don't know any better.
5. These sort of matches must be scratched on the box. Those class of people are the worst gossips. He don't think he will ever invest in those kind of securities again. Let's have these kind.

Agreement

52a. A verb agrees in number with the subject, not with a noun which intervenes between it and the subject.

Wrong: The size of the plantations vary.
Right: The size of the plantations varies.
Wrong: The increasing use of luxuries are a menace to the country.

GRAMMAR—AGREEMENT

Right: The increasing use of luxuries is a menace to the country.

Wrong: The prices of grain fluctuates in response to the demand.

Right: The prices of grain fluctuate in response to the demand. [or] The price of grain fluctuates in response to the demand.

b. The number of the verb is not affected by the addition to the subject of words introduced by *with, together with, no less than, as well as,* and the like.

Wrong: The mayor of the city, as well as several aldermen, have investigated the charges.

Right: The mayor of the city, as well as several aldermen, has investigated the charges.

c. Singular subjects joined by *or* or *nor* take a singular verb.

Wrong: Either the second or the third of the plans they have devised are acceptable.

Right: Either the second or the third of the plans they have devised is acceptable.

d. A subject consisting of two or more nouns joined by *and* takes a plural verb.

Right: The hunting and fishing are good.

e. A verb should agree in number with the subject, not with a predicate noun.

Wrong: The weak point in the team were the fielders.
Right: The weak point in the team was the fielders.
Wrong: Laziness and dissipation is the cause of his failure.
Right: Laziness and dissipation are the cause of his failure.

f. In *There is* and *There are* sentences the verb should agree in number with the noun that follows it.

GRAMMAR—*SHALL* AND *WILL*

Wrong: There is very good grounds for such a decision.
Right: There are very good grounds for such a decision.
Wrong: There was present a man, two women, and a child.
Right: There were present a man, two women, and a child.

Exercise:
1. After the accident the joys of motoring goes on as before. The sight of spring flowers please everybody.
2. He looked into the parlor where John, with Miss Gold, were sitting. The thief, accompanied by the boys, bolt into the woods.
3. Neither the bass nor the tenor are a regular member of the quartet. Hockey and curling is winter sports.
4. Of the four hundred passengers, there was fully three hundred seasick. I traveled through the fields where the timber had been cleared, and where there now remains only the smaller trees and stumps.
5. I call it a secret path because I, with three others, are the only ones who know where it is. The university, along with the better colleges, have rigid entrance requirements.

Shall and *Will, Should* and *Would*

Although there is a tendency to disregard subtle distinctions between *shall* and *will* in ordinary speech, it is desirable to preserve the more important distinctions in written discourse.

53. To express simple futurity or mere expectation, use *shall* with the first person (both singular and plural) and *will* with the second and third.

I shall go.	We shall walk.
You will play.	You will hear.
He will sing.	They will reply.

To express resolution or emphatic assurance, reverse the usage; that is, use *will* with the first person

GRAMMAR—*SHALL* AND *WILL*

(both singular and plural), and *shall* with the second and third.

I will; I tell you, I will.
You shall do what I bid.
He shall obey me.

We will not be excluded.
You shall not delay us.
They shall pay the tribute.

In asking questions, use the form expected in the answer.

"Shall I go?" I asked myself musingly. "Shall we take a walk?" "You promise. But will you pay?" "Will it rain tomorrow?"

***Should* and *would* follow the rules given for *shall* and *will*.**

Mere statement of a fact:
   I [or We] should like to go.
   You [or He or They] would of course accept the offer.

Resolution or emphatic assurance:
   I [or We] would never go under terms so degrading.
   You [or He or They] should decline; honor demands it.

***Should* has also a special use in the subjunctive (in all persons) to express a condition; and *would* has a special use (in all persons) to express a wish, or customary action.**

If it should rain, I shall not go.
If I should remain, it would probably clear off.
Would that I could swim!
He [I, We, You, They] would often sit there by the hour.

Exercise:

1. I —— [shall, will] receive a telegram, I think. I believe you —— [shall, will] enjoy your visit. Of course she —— [shall, will] tell me whether we —— [shall, will] be welcome.

2. I positively —— [shall, will] go; Vance —— [shall, will] not prevent me! You [shall, will] give me a courteous reply; I demand it. It is within my power to punish

them, and they —— [shall, will] be punished! I wonder if they —— [shall, will] be punished.

3. —— [Shall, Will] we take the right road or the left? —— [Shall, Will] you be there, rain or shine? —— [Shall, Will] you see Dutton, do you suppose? —— [Shall, Will] the faucet turn?

4. I —— [should, would] not let that fellow enter my house. You —— [should, would] pay no attention to him, nor —— [should, would] she. Men —— [should, would] prefer red, I fancy. Nothing could please them; they —— [should, would] not be satisfied.

5. If I —— [should, would] hear that, I —— [should, would] faint. If you —— [should, would] die suddenly, the insurance —— [should, would] be of great help to your family. We —— [shall, will] all die some day.

Principal Parts

54. Use the correct form of the past tense and past participle. Avoid *come, done, bursted, knowed, says* for the past tense; and [*had*] *eat*, [*had*] *froze*, [*have*] *ran*, [*has*] *went*, [*has*] *wrote*, [*are*] *suppose* for the past participle. Memorize the principal parts of difficult verbs. The principal parts are the present tense, the past tense, and the past participle. A good way to recall these is to repeat the formula: Today I *sing*; yesterday I *sang*; often in the past I have *sung*. The principal parts of *sing* are *sing, sang, sung*. A list of difficult verbs is given below.

bear	bore	borne	bite	bit	bit
		born			bitten
begin	began	begun	bleed	bled	bled
bend	bent	bent	blow	blew	blown
bid	bid	bid	break	broke	broken
	bade	bidden			

GRAMMAR—PRINCIPAL PARTS

burn	burnt	burnt	lie	lied	lied
	burned	burned	loose	loosed	loosed
burst	burst	burst	lose	lost	lost
catch	caught	caught	mean	meant	meant
choose	chose	chosen	pay	paid	paid
come	came	come	prove	proved	proved
deal	dealt	dealt	read	read	read
dive	dived	dived	rid	rid	rid
do	did	done	ride	rode	ridden
drag	dragged	dragged	ring	rang	rung
draw	drew	drawn	rise	rose	risen
dream	dreamt	dreamt	run	ran	run
	dreamed	dreamed	say	said	said
drink	drank	drunk	see	saw	seen
drive	drove	driven	set	set	set
drown	drowned	drowned	shake	shook	shaken
dwell	dwelt	dwelt	shine	shone	shone
	dwelled	dwelled	show	showed	shown
eat	ate	eaten	shrink	shrank	shrunk
fall	fell	fallen	sing	sang	sung
fight	fought	fought	sit	sat	sat
flee	fled	fled	slink	slunk	slunk
fly	flew	flown	speak	spoke	spoken
flow	flowed	flowed	spend	spent	spent
freeze	froze	frozen	spit	spit	spit
get	got	got		spat	spat
go	went	gone	steal	stole	stolen
grow	grew	grown	swear	swore	sworn
hang	hung	hung	sweep	swept	swept
hang	hanged	hanged	swim	swam	swum
hold	held	held	take	took	taken
kneel	knelt	knelt	tear	tore	torn
know	knew	known	throw	threw	thrown
lay	laid	laid	thrust	thrust	thrust
lead	led	led	tread	trod	trod
lend	lent	lent			trodden
lie	lay	lain			

GRAMMAR—TENSE, MODE, AUXILIARIES

wake	woke	waked	weave	wove	woven
	waked		weep	wept	wept
wear	wore	worn	write	wrote	written

Exercise:

1. An old trunk —— [past tense of *sit*] in a dark corner of the attic. Some one had —— [past participle of *lay*] an oil-cloth over it.
2. He —— [past tense of *do*] all he could. He —— [past tense of *lead*] his guests into the library, and they —— [past tense of *sit*] by a window.
3. I haven't —— [past participle of *shake*] hands with you yet; I'm almost —— [past participle of *freeze*]. I have —— [past participle of *ride*] twenty miles, and I have not —— [past participle of *eat*] or —— [past participle of *drink*] anything.
4. The swimmer —— [past tense of *lie*] on his side in the water, and —— [past tense of *swim*] about idly. His companion had not —— [past participle of *swim*] that day, but had —— [past participle of *sit*] reading on the shore.
5. Soon after it had —— [past participle of *begin*] to rain, the men —— [past tense of *run*] for shelter. A colt was —— [past participle of *drown*] where the embankment had —— [past participle of *burst*].

Tense, Mode, Auxiliaries

55a. In dependent clauses and infinitives, the tense is to be considered in relation to the time expressed in the principal verb.

Wrong: I intended to have gone. [The principal verb *intended* indicates a past time. In that past time I intended to do something. What? Did I intend *to go,* or *to have gone?*]

Right: I intended to go.

Wrong: We hoped that you would have come to the party. [The principal verb *hoped* indicates a past time. In that past

GRAMMAR—TENSE, MODE, AUXILIARIES

time our hope was that you *would* come, not that you *would have come*.]

Right: We hoped that you would come.

b. When narration in the past tense is interrupted for reference to a preceding occurrence, the past perfect tense is used.

Wrong: In the parlor my cousin kept a collection of animals which he shot.

Right: In the parlor my cousin kept a collection of animals which he had shot.

c. General statements equally true in the past and in the present are usually expressed in the present tense.

Faulty: He said that Venus was a planet.
Right: He said that Venus is a planet.

d. The subjunctive mode of the verb *to be* is used to express a condition contrary to fact, or a wish.

Faulty: If he was here, I should be happy.
Right: If he were here, I should be happy.
Faulty: I wish that I was a man.
Right: I wish that I were a man.

e. Use the correct auxiliary. Make sure that the tense, mode, or aspect of successive verbs is not altered without reason.

Wrong: By giving strict obedience to commands, a soldier *learns* discipline, and consequently *would have* steady nerves in time of war. [*Learns* should be followed by *will have*.]

Wrong: An automobile *should be* kept in good working order so that its life *is* lengthened. [*Should be* is properly followed by *may be*.]

Exercise:
1. I would have liked to have danced all night.
2. Many a time I have longed to have been home.

GRAMMAR—ADJECTIVE AND ADVERB

3. If the knife was mine, I should have it sharpened. I wish I was not bothered by him so often.
4. In summer the health-seekers come, in order that they might be cured of rheumatism by the radium waters.
5. It is one of these round traps, and if six mice stick their heads in at the same time, it would catch all of them.

Adjective and Adverb

56a. Do not use an adjective to modify a verb.

> Crude: He spoke slow and careful.
> Right: He spoke slowly and carefully.
> Crude: He sure did good in his classes.
> Right: He surely did well in his classes.

b. In such sentences as *He stood firm* and *The cry rang clear* the modifier should be an adjective if it refers to the subject, an adverb if it refers to the verb.

> Right: The sun shines bright on my old Kentucky home. [Here the thought is that the sun which shines is bright.]
> Right: He worked diligently. [Here the modifier refers to the manner of working rather than to the person who works. It should therefore be an adverb.]
> Right: It stood immovable. The shot rang loud. He becomes angry. The weeds grow thick. They remain obstinate. He seems intelligent.

c. After a verb pertaining to the senses, *look, sound, taste, smell, feel,* an adjective is used to denote a quality pertaining to the subject. (An adverb is used only when the reference is clearly to the verb.)

> She looks *beautiful*. [Not *beautifully*.]
> The dinner bell sounds *good*. [Not *well*.]
> My food tastes *bad*. [Not *badly*.]
> That flower smells *bad*. [Not *badly*.]

GRAMMAR—DOUBLE CAPACITY

I feel good [*in good spirits.*]
I feel well [*in good health.* An adjectival use of *well.*]
I feel bad [*in bad health or spirits.* "I feel badly" would mean "My sense of touch is impaired."]

Exercise:

1. I —— [sure, surely] feel —— [bad, badly] today. My food tastes —— [bad, badly].
2. His grades fell off —— [considerable, considerably]. He has done —— [bad, badly] in school.
3. They hired him —— [special, especially] for the Christmas holidays. No music sounds so —— [good, well] to me as Tchaikovsky's.
4. She smiled —— [joyous, joyously]. The voices grew —— [angry, angrily]. The morning broke —— [clear, clearly] and —— [bright, brightly]. The hills look —— [beautiful, beautifully].
5. Voices sound —— [queer, queerly] when you have a fever. He looks —— [weary, wearily]. He looks —— [weary, wearily] at the unanswered letters on his desk.

A Word in a Double Capacity

57. Do not use a verb, conjunction, preposition, or noun in a double capacity when one of the uses is ungrammatical.

Wrong [verb]: An opera house was built in one part of town, and two churches in another.
Right: An opera house was built in one part of town, and two churches were built in another.
Wrong [verb]: He always has and will do it.
Right: He always has done it, and always will do it.
Wrong [conjunction]: He was as old, if not older, than any other man in the community.
Right: He was as old as any other man in the community, if not older.
Wrong [preposition]: He was fond and diligent in work.

THE TERMS OF GRAMMAR

Right: He was fond of work and diligent in it.
Wrong [noun]: He is one of the most skilful, if not the most skilful, tennis players in the state.
Right: He is one of the most skilful tennis players in the state, if not the most skilful.

Exercise:

1. He was afraid and yet kind to horses.
2. He has and always will take a vacation every summer.
3. This ordinance is as severe, if not more so, than the one it replaces.
4. He was throwing stones up at the monkeys, and the monkeys cocoanuts down at him.
5. He is one of the fastest, if not the fastest, man on the track. Yet he is among the most unpopular, perhaps even the most unpopular, members of the team.

58. Parts of Speech, Other Grammatical Terms, Conjugation.

The Parts of Speech and Their Uses

Noun. A noun is a name. It may be **proper** (*Philip Watkins*), or **common**. Common nouns may be **concrete** (*man, windmill*), or **abstract** (*gratitude, nearness*). A noun applied to a group is said to be **collective** (*family, race*). The uses of a noun are: to serve as the subject of a verb, to serve as the object of a verb or a preposition, to be in apposition with another noun (Jenkins, our *coach*), to indicate possession (*Joseph's* coat of many colors); and less frequently, to serve as an adjective (the *brick* sidewalk) or adverb (John went *home*), and to indicate direct address (*Jehovah,* help us!).

Pronoun. A pronoun is a word which takes the place of a noun. It may be **personal** (*I, thou, you, he, she, it, we, they*), **relative** (*who, which, what, that, as,* and compounds *whoever, whichsoever,* etc.), **interrogative** (*who, which, what*), **demonstrative** (*this, that, these, those*), or **indefinite**

THE TERMS OF GRAMMAR

(*some, any, one, each, either, neither, none, few, all, both*, etc.). Strictly speaking, the last two groups, demonstratives and indefinites, are adjectives used as pronouns. Certain pronouns are also used as adjectives, notably the **possessives** (*my, his, their*, etc.) and the relative or interrogative *which* and *what*. The addition of *-self* to a personal pronoun forms a **reflexive pronoun** or **intensive** (I blamed *myself*. You *yourself* are at fault). A noun for which the pronoun stands is called the **antecedent**. The uses of pronouns are in general the same as those of nouns. In addition, relatives serve as connectives (the man *who* spoke), interrogatives ask questions (*what* man?), and demonstratives point out (*that* man).

Verb. A verb is a word or word-group which makes an assertion about the subject. It may express either action or mere existence. It may be **transitive** (*trans* meaning "across"; hence action carried across, requiring a receiver of the act: Brutus *stabbed* Cæsar; Cæsar is *stabbed*) or **intransitive** (not requiring a receiver of the act: Montgomery *fell*). Its meaning is dependent upon its voice, mode, and tense. Voice shows the relationship between the subject and the assertion made by the verb. The **active voice** shows the subject as actor (They *elected* Washington); the **passive voice,** as acted upon (Washington *was elected*). (A transitive verb may be active or passive, but an intransitive verb has no voice.) Mode indicates the manner of predicating an action, whether as assertion, condition, command, etc. There are three modes in English. The **indicative mode** affirms or denies (He *went*. She *did not dance*). The **subjunctive** expresses condition or wish (If he *were* older, he would be wiser. Would that I *were* there!). The **imperative** expresses command or exhortation (*Remain* there. *Go! Let* us pray). **Modal auxiliaries** with these three modes form **modal aspects** of the verb. There are as many different aspects as there are auxiliaries. Aspects are sometimes spoken of as separate modes or called collectively the "potential mode." Tense expresses the time of the action or existence. The tenses are

THE TERMS OF GRAMMAR

the **present,** the **past,** the **future** (employing the auxiliaries *shall* and *will*), the **perfect** (employing *have*), the **past perfect** (employing *had*), and the **future perfect** (employing *shall have* and *will have*). **Verbals** are certain forms of the verb used as other parts of speech (noun, adjective, adverb). For the verbal forms, infinitive, gerund, and participle, see the separate headings.

Adjective. An adjective is a word used to modify a noun or pronoun. An adjective may be **attributive** (*bright* sun, *cool-headed* adventurers) or **predicate** (The field is *broad*. The meat tastes *bad*. I want this *ready* by Christmas). Adjectives assume three forms known as degrees of comparison. The **positive degree** indicates the simple quality of the object without reference to any other. The **comparative degree** indicates that two objects are compared (Stanley is the *older* brother). The **superlative degree** indicates that three or more objects are compared (Stanley is the *oldest* child in the family) or that the speaker feels great interest or emotion (A *most excellent* record). Ordinarily *er* or *r* is added to the positive to form the comparative, and *est* or *st* to the positive to form the superlative (brave, braver, bravest). But some adjectives (sometimes those of two, and always those of more than two, syllables) prefix *more* (or *less*) to the positive to form the comparative, and *most* (or *least*) to the positive to form the superlative (beautiful, more beautiful, most beautiful). Some adjectives express qualities that do not permit comparison (*dead, four-sided, unique*).

Adverb. An adverb is a word used to modify a verb, an adjective, another adverb (She played *well;* *unusually* handsome; *very* sternly), or, more rarely, a verbal noun (Walking *fast* is good for the health) or a preposition (The ship drifted *almost* upon the breakers). Certain adverbs (*fatally, entirely*) do not logically admit of comparison. Those that do are compared like adjectives of more than two syllables (*slowly, more* or *less slowly, most* or *least slowly*).

Preposition. A preposition is a connective *placed before* a

112

THE TERMS OF GRAMMAR

substantive (called its object) in order to subordinate the substantive to some other word in a sentence (The boast *of* heraldry, the pomp *of* power. He ran *toward* the enemy *without* fear).

Conjunction. A conjunction is a word used to *join together* words, phrases, clauses, or sentences. A **coördinate conjunction** connects elements of equal rank (See 36). **Correlative conjunctions** are conjunctions used in pairs (See 31). A **subordinate conjunction** is one that connects elements unequal in rank (See 36). When a conjunction, in addition to its function as a connective, indicates a relation of time, place, or cause, it is often called a **conjunctive adverb** or **relative adverb**.

Interjection. An interjection is a word *thrown into* speech to express emotion. It has no grammatical connection with other words. (*Oh,* is that it? *Well,* I'll do it. *Hark!*)

Other Grammatical Terms

Absolute expression. An expression (usually composed of a substantive and a participle, perhaps with modifiers) which, though not formally and grammatically joined, is in thought related to the remainder of the sentence. (*The relief party having arrived,* we went home. *This disposed of,* the council proceeded to other matters. *Defeated,* he was not dismayed.)

Antecedent. A substantive to which a pronoun or participle refers. Literally, *antecedent* means *that which goes before;* but sometimes the antecedent follows the dependent word. (The *man* who hesitates is lost. Entering the store, *we* saw a barrel of apples.) *Man* is the antecedent of the pronoun *who,* and *we* is the antecedent of the participle *entering.*

Auxiliary. *Be, have, do, shall, will, ought, may, can, must, might, could, would, should,* etc., when used with participles and infinitives of other verbs, are called auxiliary verbs.

Case. The relation of a substantive to other words in the sentence as shown by inflectional form or position. The sub-

THE TERMS OF GRAMMAR

ject of a verb, or the predicate of the verb *to be*, is in the nominative case. The object of a verb or preposition, or the "assumed subject" of an infinitive, is in the objective case. A noun or pronoun which denotes possession is in the possessive case.

Clause. A portion of a sentence which contains a subject and a verb, perhaps with modifiers. The following sentence contains one dependent (subordinate) and one independent (principal) clause: *When the storm ceased, the grove was a ruin.*

Conjugation. The inflectional changes in the verb to indicate person, number, tense, voice, mode, and modal aspect.

Declension. The changes in a noun, pronoun, or adjective to indicate person, number, or case.

Ellipsis, elliptical expression. An expression partially incomplete, so that words have to be understood to complete the meaning. An idea or relation corresponding to the omitted words is present, at least vaguely, in the mind of the speaker. Elliptical sentences are usually justifiable except when the reader cannot instantly supply the understood words. Examples of proper ellipses: You are as tall as I [am tall]. Is your sister coming? I think [my sister is] not [coming]. I will go if you will [go]. [I give you] Thanks for your advice.

Gerund. A verbal in *-ing* used as a noun. (I do not object to your *telling*. His *having deserted* us makes little difference.) The gerund may be regarded as a special form of the infinitive.

Infinitive. A verbal ordinarily introduced by *to* and used as a noun (*To err* is human). In such sentences as "The road to follow is the river road," *follow* may be regarded as the noun of a phrase (compare *the road to Mandalay*), or the entire phrase may be regarded as an adjective. Similarly, in "He hastened to comply," *comply* may be regarded as a noun or *to comply* as an adverb. After certain verbs (*bid, dare, help, make, need*, etc.) the *to* is omitted from the infinitive group. (He bids me *go*. I need not *hesitate*.)

THE TERMS OF GRAMMAR

Inflection. Change in the form of a word to show a modification or shade of meaning. At a very early period in our language there was a separate form for practically every modification. Although separate forms are now less numerous, *inflection* is still a convenient term in grammar. Its scope is general: it includes the declension of nouns, the comparison of adjectives and adverbs, and the conjugation of verbs.

Modify. To be grammatically dependent upon and to limit or alter the quality of. In the expression "The very old man," *the* and *old* modify *man,* and *very* modifies *old*.

Participle. A verbal used as an adjective, or as an adjective with adverbial qualities. In the sentence "Mary, being oldest, is also the best liked," *being oldest* refers exclusively, or almost exclusively, to the subject and is therefore adjectival. In such sentences as "He fell back, exhausted" and "Running down the street, I collided with a baby carriage," the participle refers in part to the verb and is therefore adverbial as well as adjectival.

Phrase. A group of words forming a subordinate part of a sentence and not containing a subject and its verb. Examples: *With a whistle and a roar* the train arrived [prepositional phrase]. *Bowing his head,* the prisoner listened to the verdict of the jury [participial phrase]. In a loose, untechnical sense *phrase* may refer to any short group of words, even if the group includes a subject and its verb.

Predicate. The word or word-group in a sentence which makes an assertion about the subject. It consists of a finite verb with or without objects or modifiers.

Predicate adjective. An adjective in the predicate, usually linked with the subject by some form of the verb *to be* (*is, was, were,* etc.). (John is *lazy*. The soldiers were very *eager*.)

Predicate noun. A noun linked with the subject by some form of the verb *to be*. (John is *halfback*. They were our *neighbors*.)

Sentence. A sentence is a group of words containing (1) a subject (with or without modifiers) and a predicate (with or

THE TERMS OF GRAMMAR

without modifiers) and not grammatically dependent on any words outside of itself; or (2) two or more such expressions related in thought. Sentences of type 1 are simple or complex; sentences of type 2 are compound. A **simple sentence** contains one independent clause (The dog barks angrily). A **complex sentence** contains one independent clause and one or more subordinate clauses (The dog barks when the thief appears). A **compound sentence** contains two or more independent clauses (The dog barks, and the thief runs).

Substantive. A noun or a word standing in place of a noun. (The *king* summoned *parliament*. The *bravest* are the *tenderest*. *She* was inconsolable.) A **substantive phrase** is a phrase used as a noun. (*From Dan to Beersheba* is a term for the whole of Israel.) A **substantive clause** is a clause used as a noun. (*That he owed the money* is certain.)

Syntax. Construction; the grammatical relation between the words, phrases, and clauses in a sentence.

Verbal. Any form of the verb used as another part of speech. Infinitives, gerunds, and participles are verbals. They are used to express action without asserting it, and cannot, therefore, have subjects or be used as predicate verbs.

Abridged Conjugation of the verb *to take*

Indicative Mode

Tense	Active Voice	Passive Voice
Present	I take	I am taken
Past	I took	I was taken
Future	I shall (will) take	I shall (will) be taken
Perfect	I have taken	I have been taken
Past Perfect	I had taken	I had been taken
Future Perfect	I shall (will) have taken	I shall (will) have been taken

THE TERMS OF GRAMMAR

Subjunctive Mode

Tense	Active Voice	Passive Voice
Present	If I take	If I be taken
Past	If I took	If I were taken
Perfect	If I have taken	If I have been taken
Past Perfect	If I had taken	If I had been taken

Imperative Mode

Present	Take	

Modal Aspects

(Modal aspects, formed by combining auxiliaries with the main verb, give special meanings—emphatic, progressive, etc.—to the primary modes. Since there are almost as many aspects as there are auxiliaries, only a few can be enumerated here.)

		Active Voice	Passive Voice
Present Indicative	Emphatic:	I do take	
	Progressive:	I am taking	I am being taken
	Contingent:	I may take	I may be taken
	Potential:	I can take	I can be taken
	Obligative:	I must take	I must be taken
	Etc.		
Past Indicative	Emphatic:	I did take	
	Progressive:	I was taking	I was being taken
	Contingent:	I might take	I might be taken
	Potential:	I could take	I could be taken
	Obligative:	I must take	I must be taken
	Etc.		
Present Subjunctive	Emphatic:	If I do take	
	Progressive:	If I be taking	
	Contingent:	If I might take	
	Potential:	If I could take	
	Obligative:	If I must take	
	Etc.		
Present Imperative	Emphatic:	Do take	
	Progressive:	Be taking	

GRAMMAR

Verbals

Infinitive

Active Voice	Passive Voice
Present: To take	To be taken
Perfect: To have taken	To have been taken

Gerund

Present: Taking — Being taken
Perfect: Having taken — Having been taken

Participle

Present: Taking — Being taken
Past: — Taken
Perfect: Having taken — Having been taken

Exercise:

Copy a page of good prose from any book, leaving wide spaces between the lines. Indicate the part of speech of every word. This may be done by abbreviations placed beneath the words.

For example:

"Von Arden, having fallen into a very unquiet
noun   *part.*   *prep.* *art.* *adv.* *adj.*

slumber, dreamed that he was an aged man who
noun   *verb*   *conj. pers. pro. verb art. adj. noun rel. pro.*

stood beside a window."
verb *prep.* *art.* *noun*

59.   EXERCISE IN GRAMMAR

A. Case of Pronouns

Determine the correct form of the pronoun.

1. It is —— [we, us] who must pay the bills.
2. No one else plays so brilliantly as —— [she, her].
3. Is it —— [he, him]? It was —— [they, them].
4. Who would have thought of its being —— [she, her].

GRAMMAR

5. —— [Who, Whom] do you think sent me this letter? No; not —— [he, him].
6. The sponsors of the bill were —— [he, him] and his friends.
7. Mother, of course, wished —— [we, us] children to be friendly with the neighbors.
8. She walked past, leaving Pike and —— [I, me] staring in amazement.
9. She is more sprightly than —— [he, him].
10. Choose —— [whoever, whomever] is best qualified.
11. The village was a place of wonder to —— [we, us] boys in the country.
12. —— [Who, Whom] do you think left the door unlocked?
13. The speaker might object to —— [our, us] coming in late.
14. Is it —— [she, her] —— [who, whom] that organ grinder is playing for?
15. Who went with you? Was it —— [they, them]? Yes; they went with Tom and —— [I, me].
16. She will be very angry with —— [whoever, whomever] wakes the baby.
17. Don't you know —— [who, whom] you are talking to? It is —— [I, me].
18. —— [Ones, One's] word is worth as much as the —— [others, other's].
19. This letter was written by Miss Rennie, —— [who, whom], you may remember, was the stenographer of the superintendent.
20. Everybody supposes it was —— [she, her]. But between you and —— [I, me], it was —— [they, them].

B. Agreement

Determine the correct form of the verb.

1. The cause for his being warm —— [was, were] his overcoat and mittens.
2. The material of wasps' nests —— [is, are] vegetation chewed into a kind of tough paper.

GRAMMAR

3. The most common kind of golf hazards —— [is, are] piles of dirt.
4. The name commonly used in the foundry for these forms —— [is, are] "flasks".
5. Hawkeye with the two Mohicans —— [was, were] forced to leave the island.
6. Neither the gray hair nor the wrinkle —— [was, were] welcome.
7. Direct evidence as well as circumstantial —— [is, are] necessary for conviction.
8. Neither of those hogs —— [weighs, weigh] more than two hundred pounds.
9. A team consisting of eleven players —— [trots, trot] out on the field.
10. As soon as a portion of the walls —— [was, were] erected, the roof was begun.
11. A bust of Dante, together with some photographs of young men, —— [was, were] on the mantel.
12. The thing I want most —— [is, are] hot pancakes. There —— [is, are] some cooking now.
13. The rate for night messages —— [is, are] relatively cheaper than for straight telegrams.
14. There —— [is, are] bushels of hazelnuts in that patch near the river.
15. The chief, together with the oldest warriors, —— [is, are] at the head of the procession.
16. One or the other of these men —— [is, are] wrong.
17. Fits of moody depression —— [alternates, alternate] with unnatural gaiety.
18. The juice of pokeberries —— [makes, make] bright paint for bloodthirsty young braves.
19. Everybody —— [reads, read] the stories. There —— [is, are] also articles about current events.
20. See if there —— [is, are] any apples left in the trees. In all the trees there —— [is, are] only one. No; there —— [is, are] two

GRAMMAR

C. *Shall* and *Will, Should* and *Would*

Determine the correct form of the verb.

1. I —— [shall, will] perhaps have company this evening.
2. You cannot dissuade me; I —— [shall, will] resign.
3. —— [Shall, Will] we meet at the café? —— [Shall, Will] they be there?
4. They —— [shall, will] not escape me this time. I am determined they —— [shall, will] not.
5. I never —— [shall, will] go near a fly-wheel again. Still, it is hard to predict what one —— [shall, will] do.
6. As you —— [shall, will] see for yourself, the house needs painting. It —— [should, would] be painted green.
7. You —— [shall, will] get muddy if you go to dig clams. You —— [should, would] expect nothing else.
8. If the weather were fair, he —— [should, would] go down to the river. I wonder if they —— [should, would] go, if we asked them.
9. I wonder if they —— [should, would] go; it is a long way, and they are not very well.
10. If a bee —— [should, would] sting him, he —— [should, would] forget his rheumatism.
11. If I —— [should, would] have a garden, I —— [should, would] plant gaillardias.
12. You are right. I —— [should, would] do better work. I —— [shall, will] do better work.
13. Ye —— [shall, will] be exalted above all other peoples. They —— [shall, will] dwell in the house of the Lord forever.
14. —— [Shall, Will] I help you with your coat? —— [Shall, Will] I drink this chocolate now? —— [Shall, Will] you have a place closer to the fire? —— [Shall, Will] she sing again if we give her an encore?
15. Some day when we are out walking, perhaps we —— [shall, will] find a small sumac bush. I —— [shall, will] pull one up and show you what peculiar roots they have.

GRAMMAR

D. *Lie, lay; sit, set; rise, raise*

Fix in mind the following principal parts:

I lie	I lay	I have lain
I lay	I laid	I have laid
I sit	I sat	I have sat
I set	I set	I have set
I rise	I rose	I have risen
I raise	I raised	I have raised

Lie, sit, rise are used intransitively; *lay, set, raise* are used transitively. *Lay, set, raise* are causatives; that is, *to lay* means *to cause to lie*, etc.

Insert a correct form of the verb *lie* or *lay:*

1. The sailors —— in their hammocks and listened to the storm. A cat —— asleep on the floor.
2. She is forever ——ing clothes on the bed. Her hairpins are ——ing all over the dresser.
3. The jeweler —— half a dozen watches on the showcase. A locket also —— there. You dropped a paper on the floor. Never mind; let it ——.
4. Yesterday I —— here and read. The scene of the story was —— in Italy, in a village which once —— along the banks of the Arno.
5. It is time we —— plans to cultivate this land, which has —— idle too long. I have —— those sacks in the granary. They have —— out in the weather for weeks.

Insert a correct form of the verb *sit* or *set:*

6. The table is ——. We are ready to —— down and eat. —— here, Jack. Yesterday father —— here at the end. The little folks have always —— at the other end.
7. The rain is ——ting in harder than ever. Mother has —— the kettle on the stove. —— in this chair, and —— to work shelling peas.

GRAMMAR

8. For a long time Brer Rabbit had —— in the brier patch, motionless. He —— there and watched Brer Fox —— out for home.
9. He —— the chair in the corner, —— down on it, and —— to thinking of what had happened.
10. I have —— fascinated by an ant hill for hours. Of course, one must —— quietly. I suppose some people would not be interested in ——ting here alone.

Insert a correct form of the verb *rise* or *raise*.

11. No man ever —— very high by trying to —— himself by his own bootstraps.
12. It was only a small box. Pandora might have —— it with both hands. Her curiosity had ——. She —— the lid just a little.
13. At Ironton the river —— to a height of thirty feet, in spite of dykes that had been —— against it.
14. Two crooked smokes were ——ing from the hill. Perhaps some one was ——ing them as a signal. Belton —— himself in the stirrups and watched intently.
15. I wish to —— this question: is it possible to —— so much money? Mr. Chairman, I —— to a point of order.

E. Principal Parts of Verbs

In the following sentences supply the correct form of the verb.

1. They have —— [past participle of *go*] back by trolley, though they —— [past tense of *come*] in an automobile.
2. The end-gate is loose, and you may —— [*loose* or *lose*] some of your packages.
3. The pitcher had —— [past participle of *throw*] a curve which the batter had not —— [past participle of *choose*] to strike at.
4. We had scarcely —— [past participle of *speak*] three words

GRAMMAR

before the revenue officers had —— [past participle of *ride*] up.

5. The bell —— [past tense of *ring*] so furiously that we —— [past tense of *begin*] to think something was wrong.
6. The child has —— [past participle of *fall*] in the street and ——[past participle of *tear*] a hole in his clothes. No one knows how he —— [past tense of *do*] it.
7. The wind —— [past tense of *blow*] all night. The large poplar tree is —— [past participle of *break*].
8. The surveyors —— [past tense of *run*] a line to that corner. "It can't be right," — [past tense of *say*] Noolen; "I —— [past tense of *grow*] up here and I know."
9. We no sooner had —— [past participle of *speak*] and —— [past participle of *shake*] hands than he —— [past tense of *show*] me his medal, which I had not —— [past participle of *see*] before.
10. We had —— [past participle of *drive*] ten miles, and were almost —— [past participle of *freeze*]. During the last few miles we had —— [past participle of *ride*] in silence.
11. We have —— [past participle of *eat*] and —— [past participle of *drink*] nothing since morning.
12. She —— [past tense of *sing*] high C with no apparent effort. After most of the audience had —— [past participle of *go*] home I —— [past tense of *come*] to the platform and congratulated her.
13. The storm has —— [past participle of *burst*], and the river has —— [past participle of *break*] through the levee.
14. He —— [past tense of *shrink*] from the light and —— [past tense of *slink*] around the corner. I thought perhaps he had —— [past participle of *steal*] something.
15. She had —— [past participle of *take*] good care of the suit and —— [past participle of *wear*] it for two years. I would have —— [past participle of *swear*] it was new.

GRAMMAR

F. General

Improve the grammar of the following sentences.

1. He don't do his work careful.
2. She cried some, for she begun to loose heart.
3. Either the factory or a steamboat have blowed its whistle.
4. Some say that mathematics do not develop the memory.
5. The extent of his liabilities are not known.
6. He will have a hard time convincing you and I that the package's loss was accidental.
7. Each one expressed their opinion that the person best qualified for the place was me.
8. These kind of canaries are called rollers.
9. He stirred uneasy and looked furtive around him.
10. He desired to have taken up the study of law.
11. It was a chilly morning, and every one had their hands in their pocket.
12. Coates is inwardly eager, but outwardly indifferent, to praise.
13. He talks slow. She looks beautifully. The food tastes well. I feel badly.
14. The water will sure be as rough, or maybe rougher, than it was yesterday.
15. He don't feel so badly about it now. If he was given a little encouragement, it would help considerable.
16. One of the best, if not the very best, thing about the room is the wall paper.
17. These kind of seeds will not sprout good in dry weather.
18. The favorite son was Joseph, who we always remember easy enough by the many-colored coat.
19. You can make muffins as successful as me. Its her that makes mistakes; she don't understand cooking. I tell her plain how to do, but her cooking doesn't taste well.
20. Mexican soldiers salute scrupulous with the open palm toward you. That's to prove they mean good by you and haven't any weapons concealed.

DICTION

Wordiness

60. Avoid wordiness. Strike out words not essential to the thought.

Roundabout impersonal construction: There are many interesting things which may be seen in New York. [12 words.]

Better: Many interesting things may be seen in New York. [9 words.]

Clause to be reduced to a phrase: The skeleton which stood in the office of Dr. Willard was terrifying to little Cecil. [15 words.]

Right: The skeleton in Dr. Willard's office was terrifying to little Cecil. [11 words.]

Clause and phrase each to be reduced to a word: Men who cared only for their individual interests were now in a state of discouragement. [15 words.]

Right: Selfish men were now discouraged. [5 words.]

Separate predication in excess: That day I was shocking wheat behind the binder. Shocking wheat behind the binder was my usual job in harvest. That day while I was working at this job, I found a nest full of partridge eggs. [37 words.]

Right: That day, while shocking wheat behind the binder, my usual job in harvest, I found a nest full of partridge eggs. [21 words.]

Ponderous scientific terms for simple ideas: Since, according to the physicists, the per cent of efficiency of a machine is equal to the amount of useful work performed, divided by the amount of energy put in, it naturally follows that in all human activities, unnecessary friction, since it lowers the amount of nervous energy, is going to lower the per cent of efficiency. While we may never reach an astonishing degree of efficiency by economizing nervous energy, nevertheless, if we consistently and perseveringly try to spare ourselves all

DICTION—WORDINESS

unnecessary labor and exertion, we shall have an abundant supply of energy to direct into channels of usefulness. [100 words.]

Right: If we economize our strength, we can make our actions more efficient and useful. [14 words.]

Inflated writing: She was supreme in beauty among the daughters of Eve whom his ravished eyes had hitherto beheld. [17 words.]

Right: She was the most beautiful woman he had ever seen. [10 words.]

Note.—A special form of wordiness is tautology—the useless repetition of an idea in different words.

Gross tautology: He had an entire monopoly of the whole fruit trade. [This is like saying "black blackbird."]
Right: He had a monopoly of the fruit trade.

Tautological expressions:

this here	connect up
where at	meet up with
return back	combined together
ascend up	perfectly all right
repeat again	utter absence of
biography of his life	quite round
good benefits	circular in form
fellow playmates	big in size
Hallowe'en evening	many in number
important essentials	strict accuracy
indorse on the back	absolutely annihilated
necessary requisite	still continue to
total effect of all this	absolutely new creation

Exercise:

1. When I was in Las Vegas, I had a rather peculiar thing happen to me. There were ten of us boys in number, and we started out one fine morning.

DICTION—TRITENESS

2. The army retreated back to its base. There it renewed its courage again.
3. John Panian and I hauled ties from Stonewall to Trinidad. Stonewall is a lumber camp which is about forty miles from Trinidad.
4. Every morning the garbage wagon came for the garbage. Godkin always placed the can at the curb for it. That morning, following his custom, he placed the can at the curb. But that morning the garbage wagon failed to come for the garbage.
5. I hereby wish to make an application for a position as a stenographer in your office. I am a young woman eighteen years of age, and I have had very little or no experience. In my opinion, I believe that I can do satisfactory work. For references I refer you to the names of the men listed below.

Triteness

61. Avoid trite or hackneyed expressions. Such expressions may be tags from everyday speech (*the worse for wear, had the time of my life*); or stale phrases from newspapers (*taken into custody, the officiating clergyman*); or humorous substitutions (*ferocious canine, paternal ancestor*); or forced synonyms (*gridiron heroes, the Hoosier metropolis*); or conventional fine writing (*reigns supreme, wind kissed the tree-tops*); or oft-repeated euphemisms (*limb* for *leg, pass away* for *die*); or overworked quotations from literature (*monarch of all I survey, footprints on the sands of time*).

List of trite expressions:

along these lines	sadder but wiser
meets the eye	did justice to a dinner
feathered songsters	a goodly number
a long-felt want	budding genius

DICTION—THE EXACT WORD

the last sad rites
launched into eternity
last but not least
doomed to disappointment
at one fell swoop
trees stood like sentinels
method in his madness
sun-kissed meadows
tired but happy
hoping you are the same
nipped in the bud
the happy pair
seething mass of humanity
specimen of humanity
with bated breath
green with envy
beggars description
a dull thud
silence broken only by
wended their way
abreast of the times
the proud possessor
too full for utterance
a pugilistic encounter
conspicuous by its absence
with whom they come in contact
exception proves the rule
favor with a selection
as luck would have it
more easily imagined than described
where ignorance is bliss

Exercise:

1. We partook of refreshments with some of the fair sex.
2. The happy pair left for the Blue Grass State amid the plaudits of hosts of friends.
3. All nature seemed to smile; a lovely breeze crept through the valley, and the tall sentinel trees whispered together.
4. Last night a motorman on our local rapid transit engaged in a fistic encounter with one of the minions of the law.
5. The speakers from the University of Pittsburg were to arrive over the Pennsylvania Line, but on account of a breakdown on the Panhandle route the spellbinders from the Smoky City were unavoidably detained.

The Exact Word

Find the exact word. Do not be content with a loose meaning. Seek the verb, the noun, the adjective, the adverb, or the phrase which expresses your thought with precision. Such words as *said, proposi-*

DICTION—THE EXACT WORD

tion, and *nice* are often used too loosely. Observe the possible gain in definiteness by substitution.

For *said* (verb): *declared, related, insisted, exclaimed, added, repeated, replied, admitted, commented, corrected, protested, explained, besought, interrupted, inquired, stammered, sighed, murmured,* or *thundered.*

For *proposition* (noun): *transaction, undertaking, venture, recourse, suggestion, overture, proposal, proffer, convenience, difficulty, thesis,* or *doctrine.*

For *nice* (adjective): *discriminating, precise, fastidious, dainty, neat, pretty, pleasant, fragrant, delicious, well-behaved, good, fine,* or *moral.*

Inexact verb: He had not sufficiently *regarded* the difficulties of the task [Use *considered*].

Inexact noun: Promptness is an *item* which a manager should possess [Use *quality*].

Inexact adjective: He looked *awfully funny* when I told him he had made a mistake [Use *surprised*].

Inexact phrasing throughout: Health is first in every line of activity. A man who has it does not hold it with enough respect, and make efforts enough to keep it.

Right: Health is indispensable to success in any work. Even those who have it do not realize its value.

Exercise:

1. They were envious of the industry he had performed. It was an old building fixed into a garage.
2. Pythagoras was a mathematician, and made many valuable discoveries along those lines.
3. Breathing contracts more diseases than any other form by which microörganisms enter the body.
4. When a freshman starts school in September he is pretty keen. We boys all want to complete school, but we have very little finances left.
5. Country people are very energetic, but are backward in leading out at public meetings. Whenever the environment of

DICTION—CONCRETENESS—SOUND

the farm equals that of the city, no boy will care to leave his country home.

Concreteness

3. Concrete words are often more effective than vague, general, or abstract words.

Not specific: She held herself aloof from her brothers' games and amusements.

Concrete: She never played soldier or sailed paper boats with her brothers.

No appeal to the senses: I liked to watch the servant girl as she moved about the kitchen, preparing our morning repast.

Concrete: I liked to watch Norah as she fried our crisp breakfast bacon and browned our buckwheat cakes.

Flat, not readily visualized: The first inhabitants overcame the barriers to settlement about a century ago.

Concrete: Rough backwoodsmen broke through the underbrush and swamp-land a century ago.

Exercise:

1. A man came down the road in a vehicle.
2. The old negro woman wore a costume of extraordinary colors.
3. The horse went carefully with the children on his back.
4. In the spring nature shows in various ways that life is being renewed.
5. He could tell from the sounds in the next room that a meal was being prepared.

Sound

4. Avoid the frequent repetition of a sound, especially if it be harsh or unpleasant.

Bad: He is an exceedingly orderly secretary.

Better: As a secretary he is very systematic. [Or] The secretary is very systematic.

DICTION—SUBTLE VIOLATIONS

Bad: Immediately the squirrel hid himself behind the hickory tree.
Better: Immediately the squirrel dodged behind the hickory tree.
Unfortunate rime: Bert did not dare to go home with wet hair.
Better: Bert did not dare to go home with his hair wet. [Or] Bert was afraid to go home with wet hair.

Exercise:
1. His life is a miserable fizzle.
2. Paul's goal is only to own gold.
3. Modern surgery surely prevents many a tragedy.
4. The side of the egg he descried was well fried.
5. They were laughing and chattering all during the dancing.

Subtle Violations of Good Use:
Faulty Idioms, Colloquialisms

65. Avoid subtle violations of good use, particularly (a) faulty idioms and (b) colloquialisms.

a. Make your expression conform to English idiom. A faulty idiom is an expression which, though correct in grammar and general meaning, combines words in a manner contrary to usage. Idioms are established by custom, and cannot be explained by logical rules. "I enjoy to read" is wrong, not because the words offend logic or grammar, but merely because people do not instinctively make that combination of words. "I like to read" and "I enjoy reading" are good idioms.

Faulty Idioms	Correct Idioms
in the city Toledo	in the city of Toledo
in the year of 1920	in the year 1920
I hope you a good time	I wish you a good time

DICTION—SUBTLE VIOLATIONS

Faulty Idioms	Correct Idioms
the Rev. Hopkins	the Reverend Mr. Hopkins
possessed with ability	possessed of ability
stay to home	stay at home
different than	different from
independent from	independent of
in search for	in search of
remember of	remember

Observe that many idioms are concerned with prepositions. Make sure that a verb or adjective is accompanied by the right preposition. Study the following list of correct idioms:

accused of (a theft)
accused by (a person)
accord with (a person)
agree with (a person)
agree to (a proposal)
agreeable to
angry at (a condition)
angry with (a person)
careful about (an affair)
careful of (one's money)
comply with
convenient to (a person)
convenient for (a purpose)
correspond to (things)
correspond with (persons)
dissent from
enamored of
entrust to
free from
listen to
part from (a person)
part with (a thing)
pleased with
resolve on
sympathize with
take exception to
wait for
wait on (a customer)

b. Do not carry the standards of conversation into formal writing. Colloquial usage is more free than literary usage. The colloquial sentence *That's the man I talked with* becomes in writing *That is the man with whom I talked*. The colloquial sentence *It was a cold day but there wasn't any wind blowing* is a loose string of

DICTION—GROSS VIOLATIONS

words. Written discourse requires greater tension and more care in subordinating minor ideas: *The day, though cold, was still.* Contractions are proper in conversation, and in personal or informal writing. In formal writing they are not appropriate. And do not let such expressions as *He doesn't, We aren't, It's proved,* used in talk by careful speakers, mislead you into expressions like *He don't, We ain't, It's proven,* which violate even colloquial good use.

Exercise:
1. Do whichever you rather. Before beginning to speak be sure if you have your thoughts in order.
2. Lincoln is noted very extensively by his letters and speeches. My high school career was no different than the average person's.
3. The Rev. Dodsley said the incident had a close resemblance for one he had witnessed in his boyhood.
4. The secretary's the only one he had much respect toward. He wasn't much averse about going; was he?
5. The ship couldn't put to sea since so many sailors were prejudiced with sailing in her, and the captain said he'd resign if the owners would profit from that action, but they wouldn't admit that he was deserving for such treatment at their hands.

Gross Violations of Good Use:

Barbarisms, Improprieties, Slang

66. Avoid gross violations of good use, particularly (a) barbarisms, (b) improprieties, and (c) slang.

a. Barbarisms are distortions of words in good use, or coinages for which there is no need. Examples: *to*

DICTION—GROSS VIOLATIONS

concertize, to burgle or *burglarize, to jell, alright, a-plenty, most* (for *almost*), *performess, fake, pep, tasty, illy, complected, undoubtably, nowheres, soph, lab, gents.*

2. **Improprieties are words wrenched from one part of speech to another, or made to perform an unnatural service.** Examples: *to suspicion, to gesture, to suicide, a steal, a try, a go, an invite, the eats, humans, some* or *real* or *swell* (as adverbs), *like* (as a conjunction).

3. **Slang is speech consisting either of uncouth expressions of illiterate origin, or of legitimate expressions used in grotesque or irregular senses.** Though sometimes (witness eighteenth century *mob*, and nineteenth century *buncombe*) it satisfies a real need and becomes established in the language, in most instances it is short-lived (witness the thieves' talk in *Oliver Twist*, or passages from any comic opera song popular five years ago). Vicious types of slang are:

Expressions of vulgar origin (from criminal classes, the prize ring, the vaudeville circuit, etc.): *get pinched, down and out, took the count, bum hunch, nix on the comedy stuff, get across.*

Language strained or distorted for novel effect: *performed the feed act at a bang-up gastronomic emporium, bingled a tall drive that made the horsehide ramble out into center garden.*

Blanket expressions used as substitutes for thinking: *corking, stunning, ain't it fierce? can you beat it? going some, just so I get by with it.*

The use of the last-named type is most to be regretted. It leads to a mental habit of phonographic repetition, with no resort to independent thinking. If a man really desires

DICTION—WORDS OFTEN CONFUSED

to use slang, let him invent new expressions every day, and make them fit the specific occasion.

Exercise:

1. The cop gave me the once-over when I parked my Tin Lizzie there. But I got by with it.
2. Nichols accepted the invite, and got outside of more eats than I thought a human could.
3. The hotel slept three men in a room. The grub was plenty good, alright, if you felt real hungry.
4. The movie crowds began to exit to the street. In every gilded pleasure-house the celluloid passions of the screen had come to their kissful conclusion.
5. Aren't you crazy about the soph history course? So am I —not. The prof is killing. We just scream. The hour is endless, and there he stands, big as outdoors. And that exam, Mabel, it was absolutely wild. It is just terrible. I would die if he called on me. To waste those perfectly good hours, when we might be putting on a tea, or something. You know, the last reception, a frosh tried to speak to me. The dance was just perfect. It was just fine. And Oh, say! let me tell you about the stunt we pulled.

Words Often Confused in Meaning

67. Do not confuse or interchange the meanings of the following words:

Accept and *except*. *Accept* means *to receive;* *except* as a verb means *to exclude* and as a preposition means *with the exception of.*

Affect and *effect*. *Affect* is not used as a noun; *effect* as a noun means *result*. As verbs, *affect* means *to influence in part;* *effect* means *to accomplish totally*. "His story affected me deeply." "The Russians effected a revolution." *Affect* also has a special meaning *to feign*. "She had an affected manner."

DICTION—WORDS OFTEN CONFUSED

Allusion and illusion. *Allusion* means a *reference;* *illusion* means a *deceptive appearance.* "A Biblical allusion." "An optical illusion."

Already and all ready. *Already* means *by this time* or *beforehand;* *all ready* means *wholly ready.* "I have already invited him." "Dinner is all ready." "We are all ready for dinner."

Altogether and all together. *Altogether* means *wholly, entirely;* *all together* means *collectively, in a group.* "He is altogether honest." "The King sent the people all together into exile."

Can and may. *Can* means *to be able;* *may* means *to have permission.* *Can* for *may* has a certain colloquial standing, but is condemned by literary usage.

Credible and creditable. *Credible* means *capable or worthy of belief;* *creditable* means *meritorious.*

Emigrate and immigrate. *Emigrate* means *to go out from a country;* *immigrate* means *to enter into a country.* The same man may be an *emigrant* when he leaves Europe, and an *immigrant* when he enters America.

Healthy and healthful. *Healthy* means *having health;* *healthful* means *giving health.* "Milk is healthful." "The climate of Colorado is healthful." "The boy is healthy."

Hanged and hung. *Hanged* is the correct past tense of *hang* in the sense *put to death, hanged on the gallows;* *hung* is the correct past tense for the general meaning *suspended.*

Hygienic and sanitary. Both words mean *pertaining to health.* *Hygienic* is used when the condition is a matter of personal habits or rules; *sanitary* is used when the condition is a matter of surroundings (water supply, food supply, sewage disposal, etc.) or the relations of numbers of people.

Instants and instance. *Instants* means *small portions of time;* *instance* means *an example.*

Later and latter. *Later* means *more late;* *latter* means *the second in a series of two.* "The latter" is used in conjunction with the phrase "the former."

137

DICTION—WORDS OFTEN CONFUSED

Lead and led. *Led* is the past tense of the verb *to lead*. *Lead* is the present tense.

Learn and teach. *Learn* means *to get knowledge of*; *teach* means *to give knowledge of* or *to*. "The instructor *teaches* (not *learns*) me physics." "He learns his lessons easily."

Leave and let. *Leave* means *to abandon*; *let* means *to permit*.

Less and fewer. *Less* refers to quantity; *fewer* refers to number. "He has *fewer* (not *less*) horses than he needs."

Liable, likely and apt. *Likely* merely predicts; *liable* conveys the additional idea of harm or responsibility. *Apt* applies usually to persons, in the sense of *having natural capability*, and sometimes to things, in the sense of *fitting, appropriate*. "It is likely to be a pleasant day." "I fear it is liable to rain." "He is liable for damages." "He is an apt lad at his books." "That is an apt phrase."

Lie and lay. *Lay*, a transitive verb, means *to cause to lie*. "I lay the book on the table and it lies there." "Now I lay me down to sleep." A source of confusion between the two words is that the past tense of *lie* is *lay*:

I lie down to sleep.	I lay the book on the table.
I lay there yesterday.	I laid it there yesterday.
I have lain here for hours.	I have laid it there many times.

Like and as or as if. *Like* is in good use as a preposition, and may be followed by a noun; *as* is in good use as a conjunction, and may be followed by a clause. "He is tall like his father." "He is tall, as his father is." "It looks *as if* (not *like*) it were going to rain."

Lose and loose. *Lose* means *to cease having*; *loose* as a verb means *to set free*, and as an adjective, *free, not bound*.

Majority and plurality. In a loose sense, *majority* means the *greater part*. More strictly, it means the number by which votes cast for one candidate exceed those of the opposition. A *plurality* is the excess of votes received by one candidate over his nearest competitor. In an election A receives 500

DICTION—WORDS OFTEN CONFUSED

votes; B, 400 votes; and C, 300 votes. A has a plurality of 100, but no majority.

Practical and practicable. *Practical* means *not theoretical; practicable* means *capable of being put into practice.* "A practical man." "The arrangement is practicable."

Principal and principle. *Principal* as an adjective means *chief* or *leading; principle* as a noun means a *general truth. Principal* as a noun means a *sum of money,* or the *chief official of a school.*

Proof and evidence. In a law court, *proof* is *evidence sufficient to establish a fact; evidence* is *whatever is brought forward in an attempt to establish a fact.* "The evidence against the prisoner was extensive, but hardly proof of his guilt." In ordinary speech, *proof* is sometimes loosely used as a synonym for *evidence.*

Pseudo- and quasi-. As a prefix, *pseudo-* means *false; quasi-* means literally *as if,* hence *seeming, so-called.* "Phrenology is a pseudo-science." "A quasi-evolutionary doctrine."

Quiet and quite. *Quiet* is an adjective meaning *calm, not noisy; quite* is an adverb meaning *entirely.*

Respectfully and respectively. *Respectfully* means *in a courteous manner; respectively* means *in a way proper to each.* "Yours *respectfully*" (not *respectively*). "He handed the commissions to Gray and Hodgins respectively."

Rise and raise. *Rise* is an intransitive verb; *raise* is a transitive verb. "I rise to go home." "I raise vegetables." "I raise the stone from the ground."

Sit and set. *Set,* a transitive verb, means *to cause to sit.* "He sets it in the corner and it sits there." The past tense of *sit* is *sat.*

I sit down.	I always set it in its place.
He sat in this very chair.	I set it in its place yesterday.
He has sat there an hour.	I have always set it just here.

Two special expressions, "The hen sets" and "The sun (moon, star) sets," though sometimes attacked as illogical, are justified by usage.

GLOSSARY OF FAULTY DICTION

Stationary and stationery. *Stationary* is an adjective meaning *fixed;* *stationery* is a noun meaning *writing materials.*

Statue, stature, and statute. *Statue* means a *carved or moulded figure;* *stature* means *height;* *statute* means a *law.*

Exercise:

1. No one —— [accept, except] Renfrew had the least idea what the —— [affect, effect] of the petition would be. It was —— [liable, likely] to —— [affect, effect] an improvement, but was —— [quiet, quite] as —— [liable, likely] to do the opposite.
2. For a while the verdict —— [hanged, hung] in uncertainty. —— [Later, Latter] the former of the two murderers was acquitted, and the —— [later, latter] was sentenced to be —— [hanged, hung]. This —— [learned, taught] me how subtle are the distinctions the law makes.
3. We went —— [altogether, all together] to see the doctor. But we were not —— [altogether, all together] pleased with his verdict. Pure air is —— [healthful, healthy]. His outdoor life has made him —— [healthful, healthy]. Kissing the baby is —— [unhygienic, unsanitary].
4. He has had much —— [practical, practicable] experience. I believe his plan for a sea-level canal is —— [practical, practicable]. It looks —— [like, as if] he were the man we want.
5. I asked the —— [principal, principle], "—— [Can, May] we have a holiday?" He —— [sit, sat, set] there quietly and said, "No. It's a matter of —— [principal, principle]." The only thing left for me was to —— [sit, set] down.

Glossary of Faulty Diction

68. Avoid faulty diction.

Accidently. No such word exists. Use *accidentally.*

Ad (for *advertisement*). Avoid in formal writing and speaking.

GLOSSARY OF FAULTY DICTION

Ain't. Never correct. Say *I'm not, you [we, they] aren't, he [she, it] isn't.*

All the farther, all the faster. Crude. Use *as far as, as fast as*, in such sentences as "This is all the farther I can go."

Alright. No such word exists. Use *all right.*

Anyplace. No such word exists. Use *any place.*

As. (a) Incorrect in the sense of *that* or *whether.* "I don't know *whether* (not *as*) I can tell you." "Not *that* (not *as*) I know." (b) *As . . . as* are correlatives. *Than* must not replace the second *as.* Right: "As good as or better than his neighbors." "As good as his neighbors, or better [than they]." See 57.

Auto. An abbreviation not desirable in formal writing.

Awful. Means *filling with awe* or *filled with awe.* Do not use in the sense of *uncivil, serious,* or *ludicrous,* or (in the adverbial form) in the sense of *very, extremely.*

Balance. Incorrect when used in the sense of *remainder.*

Because. Not to be used for *the fact that.* "The fact that (not *because*) he is absent is no reason why we should not proceed." See 5.

Between. Used of two persons or things. Not to be confused with *among,* which is used of more than two.

Blame on. A crudity for *put the blame on* or *blame.* Faulty: "Don't blame it on me." Better: "Don't blame me."

Borned. A monstrosity for *born.* "I was *born* (not *borned*) in 1899."

Bursted. The past tense of *burst* is the same as the present.

Bust or busted. Vulgar for *burst.* Right: "The balloon burst." "The bank failed."

But what. *That* is often preferable. "I do not doubt *that* (not *but what*) he is honest."

Canine. An adjective. Not in good use as a noun.

Cannot help but. A confusion of *can but* and *cannot help.* "I can but believe you"; or "I cannot help believing you"; not "I cannot help but believe you." See 34.

Caused by. To be used only when it refers definitely to a

GLOSSARY OF FAULTY DICTION

noun. Wrong: "He was disappointed, caused by the lateness of the train." The noun *disappointment* should be used instead of the verb *disappointed*. Then *caused* will have a definite reference. Right: "His disappointment was caused by the lateness of the train." See 23.

Claim. Means *to demand as a right*. Incorrect for *maintain* or *assert*.

Considerable. An adjective, not an adverb. "He talked *considerably* (not *considerable*) about it."

Could of. An illiterate form arising from slovenly pronunciation. Use *could have*. Avoid also *may of, must of, would of,* etc.

Data. Plural. The singular (seldom used) is *datum*. Compare *stratum, strata; erratum, errata*.

Demean. Means *to conduct oneself*, not *to lower* or *to degrade*.

Different than. *Different from* is to be preferred. *Than* is a conjunction. The idea of separation implied in *different* calls for a preposition, rather than a word of comparison.

Disremember. Not in good use.

Done. A gross error when used as the past tense of *do*, or as an adverb meaning *already*. "I did it (not *I done it*)." "I've *already* (not *done*) got my lessons."

Don't. A contraction for *do not;* never to be used for *does not*. The contraction of *does not* is *doesn't*. See 51d.

Drownded. Vulgar for *drowned*.

Due to. To be used only when it refers definitely to a noun. Faulty: "He refused the offer, due to his father's opposition." Right: "His refusal of the offer was due to his father's opposition." The noun *refusal* should be used instead of the verb *refused*. Then *due* will have a definite reference. See 5.

Enthuse. Not in good use.

Etc. An abbreviation for the Latin *et cetera*, meaning *and other* [things]. *Et* means *and*. *And etc.* is therefore grossly incorrect. Do not write *ect*.

142

GLOSSARY OF FAULTY DICTION

Expect. Means *to look forward to*. Hardly correct in the sense of *suppose*.

Fine. Use cautiously as an adjective, and not at all as an adverb. Seek the exact word. See 62.

Former. Means the first or first named of two. Not to be used when more than two have been named. The corresponding word is *latter*.

For to. Incorrect for *to*. "I want *you* (not *for you*) to listen carefully." "He made up his mind *to* (not *for to*) accept."

Gent. A vulgar abbreviation of *gentleman*.

Good. An adjective, not an adverb. Wrong: "He did good in mathematics." Right: "He did well in mathematics." "He did good work in mathematics."

Gotten. An old form now usually replaced by *got* except in such expressions as *ill-gotten gains*.

Guess. Expresses conjecture. Not to be used in formal composition for *think, suppose,* or *expect*.

Had of. Illiterate. "I wish I *had known* (not *had of known*) about it."

Had ought. A vulgarism. "He *ought* (not *had ought*) to have resigned." "We *oughtn't* (not *hadn't ought*) to make this error."

Hardly. Not to be used with a negative. See 34.

Home. Do not use when you mean simply *house*.

Human or humans. Not in good use as a noun. Say *human being*. Right: "The house was not fit for *human beings* (not *humans*) to live in."

If. Do not use for *whether*. "I can't say *whether* (not *if*) the laundry will be finished today."

In. Often misused for *into*. "He jumped *into* (not *in*) the pond."

It's. Means *it is;* not to be written for the possessive *its*.

Kind of. (a) Should not modify adjectives or verbs. "He was *somewhat* (not *kind of*) lean." "She *partly suspected* (not *She kind of suspected*) what was going on." (b) When

GLOSSARY OF FAULTY DICTION

using with a noun, do not follow by *a*. "That kind of man"; not "That kind of a man."

Like. To be followed by a substantive; never by a substantive and a verb. "He ran like a deer." "Do *as* (not *like*) I do." "She felt *as if* (not *like*) she was going to faint." *Like* is a preposition; *as* is a conjunction.

Literally. Do not use where you plainly do not mean it, as in the sentence, "I was literally tickled to death."

Loan. *Lend* is in better use as a verb.

Locate. Do not use for *settle* or *establish oneself*.

Lose out. Not used in formal writing. Say *lose*.

Lots of. A mercantile term which has a dubious colloquial standing. Not in good literary use for *many* or *much*.

Might of. A vulgarism for *might have*.

Most. Do not use for *almost*. "*Almost* (not *most*) all."

Myself. Intensive or reflexive; do not use when the simple personal pronoun would suffice. "I saw them myself." "Some friends and *I* (not *myself*) went walking."

Neither. Used with *nor*, and not with *or*. "Neither the man whom his associates had suspected *nor* (not *or*) the one whom the police had arrested was the criminal." "She could neither paint a good picture *nor* (not *or*) play the violin well."

Nice. Means *delicate* or *precise*. *Nice* is used in a loose colloquial way to indicate general approval, but should not be so used in formal writing. Right: "He displayed nice judgment." "We had a *pleasant* (not *nice*) time." See 62.

Nowhere near. Vulgar for *not nearly*.

Nowheres. Vulgar.

O and Oh. *O* is used with a noun in direct address; it is not separated from the noun by any marks of punctuation. *Oh* is used as an interjection; it is followed by a comma or an exclamation point. "Hear, O king, what thy servants would say." "Oh, dear!"

Of. Do not use for *have* in such combinations as *should have, may have, ought to have*.

GLOSSARY OF FAULTY DICTION

Off of. Use *off* alone. "He jumped *off* (not *off of*) the platform."

Onto. *On, upon,* or *on to* is preferable.

Ought to of. A vulgarism for *ought to have*.

Over with. Crude for *over*.

Pants. *Trousers* is the approved term in literary usage. *Pants* (from *pantaloons*) has found some degree of colloquial and commercial acceptance.

Party. Not to be used for *person*, except in legal phrases.

Phenomena. Plural. "It was an interesting *phenomenon* (not *phenomena*)."

Phone. A contraction not employed in formal writing. Say *telephone*.

Plenty. A noun; not in good use as an adjective or an adverb. "He had *plenty of* (not *plenty*) resources." "He had *resources in plenty* (not *resources plenty*)."

Proposition. Means a *thing proposed*. Do not use loosely, as in the sentence: "A berth on a Pullman is a good proposition during a railway journey at night." See 62.

Proven. Prefer *proved*.

Providing. Prefer *provided* in such expressions as "I will vote for him *provided* (not *providing*) he is a candidate."

Quite a. Colloquial in such expressions as *quite a while, quite a few, quite a number*.

Raise. *Rear* or *bring up* is preferable in speaking of children. "She *reared* (not *raised*) seven children."

Rarely ever. Crude for *rarely, hardly ever*.

Real. Crude for *very* or *really*. "She was *very* (not *real*) intelligent." "He was *really* (not *real*) brave."

Remember of. Not to be used for *remember*.

Right smart and **Right smart of.** Extremely vulgar.

Same. No longer used as a pronoun except in legal documents. "He saw her drop the purse and restored *it* (not *the same*) to her."

Scarcely. Not to be used with a negative. See 34.

Seldom ever. Crude for *seldom, hardly ever*.

GLOSSARY OF FAULTY DICTION

Shall. Do not confuse with *will*. See 53.

Sight. *A sight* or *a sight of* is very crude for *many, much, a great deal of*. "A great many (not *a sight*) of them."

So. Not incorrect, but loose, vague, and often unnecessary. (a) As an intensive, the frequent use of *so* has been christened "the feminine demonstrative". Hackneyed: "I was so surprised." Better: "I was much surprised." Or, "I was surprised." (b) As a connective, the frequent use of *so* is a mark of amateurishness. See 36 Note.

Some. Not to be used as an adverb. "She was *somewhat* (not *some*) better the next day." Wrong: "He studied some that night." Right: "He did some studying that night."

Somewheres. Very crude. Use *somewhere*.

Species. Has the same form in singular and plural. "He discovered a new *species* (not *specie*) of sunflower."

Such. (a) To be completed by *that*, rather than by *so that*, when a result clause follows. "There was such a crowd *that* (not *so that*) he did not find his friends." (b) To be completed by *as*, rather than by *that, who*, or *which*, when a relative clause follows. "I will accept such arrangements *as* (not *that*) may be made." "He called upon such soldiers *as* (not *who*) would volunteer for this service to step forward."

Superior than. Not in good use for *superior to*.

Sure. Avoid the crude adverbial use. "It *surely* (not *sure*) was pleasant." In answer to the question, "Will you go?" either *sure* or *surely* is correct, though *surely* is preferred. "[To be] sure." "[You may be] sure." "[I will] surely [go]."

Suspicion. A noun. Never to be used as a verb.

Take and. Often unnecessary, sometimes crude. Redundant: "He took the ax and sharpened it." Better: "He sharpened the ax." Crude: "He took and nailed up the box." Better: "He nailed up the box."

Tend. In the sense *to look after*, takes a direct object without an interposed *to*. *Attend*, however, is followed by *to*. "The

GLOSSARY OF FAULTY DICTION

milliner's assistant *tends* (not *tends to*) the shop." "I shall *attend to* your wants in a moment."

That there. Do not use for *that*. "I want *that* (not *that there*) box of berries."

Them. Not to be used as an adjective. "*Those* (not *them*) boys."

There were or **There was.** Avoid the unnecessary use. Crude: "There were seventeen senators voted for the bill." Better: "Seventeen senators voted for the bill."

These sort, These kind. Ungrammatical. See 51b.

This here. Do not use for *this*.

Those. Do not carelessly omit a relative clause after *those*. Faulty: "He is one of those talebearers." Better: "He is a talebearer." [Or] "He is one of those talebearers whom everybody dislikes."

Those kind, those sort. Ungrammatical. See 51b.

Till. Do not carelessly misuse for *when*. "I had scarcely strapped on my skates *when* (not *till*) Henry fell through an air hole."

Transpire. Means *to give forth* or *to become known*, not *to occur*. "The secret *transpired*." "The sale of the property *occurred* (not *transpired*) last Thursday."

Try. A verb, not a noun.

Unique. Means *alone of its kind*, not *odd* or *unusual*.

United States. Ordinarily preceded by *the*. "The United States raised a large army." (Not "United States raised a large army.")

Up. Do not needlessly insert after such verbs as *end, rest, settle*.

Used to could. Very crude. Say *used to be able* or *once could*.

Very. Accompanied by *much* when used with the past participle. "He was *very much* (not *very*) pleased with his reception."

Want to. Not to be used in the sense of *should, had better*. "You *should* (not *want to*) keep in good physical condition."

GLOSSARY OF FAULTY DICTION

Way. Not to be used for *away*. "*Away* (not *way*) down the street."

Ways. Not to be used for *way* in referring to distance. "A little *way* (not *ways*)."

When. (a) Not to be used for *that* in such a sentence as "It was in the afternoon that the races began." (b) A *when* clause is not to be used as a predicate noun. See 6.

Where. (a) Not to be used for *that* in such a sentence as "I see in the paper that our team lost the game." (b) A *where* clause is not to be used as a predicate noun. See 6.

Where at. Vulgar. "Where is he? (not *Where is he at?*)"

Which. Do not use for *who* or *that* in referring to persons. "The friends *who* (not *which*) had loved him in his boyhood were still faithful to him."

Who. Do not use unnecessarily for *which* or *that* in referring to animals or things. Do not use the possessive form *whose* for *of which* unless the sentence is so turned as practically to require the substitution.

Will. Do not confuse with *shall*. See 53.

Win out. Not used in formal writing or speaking.

Woods. The singular form should ordinarily be preferred. "*A wood* (not *A woods*)."

Would have. Do not use for *had* in *if* clauses. "If you *had* (not *would have*) spoken boldly, he would have granted your request."

Would of. A vulgarism for *would have*.

You was. Use *You were* in both singular and plural.

Yourself. Intensive or reflexive; do not use when the personal pronoun would suffice. "*You* (not *Yourself*) and your family must come."

Exercise:

1. That was all the faster the muskrat could run. He was not one of those running kind.
2. If the party I was talking with had of known what you phoned me, he wouldn't scarcely of said what he did.
3. There were nowheres near a hundred trees in the orchard.

DICTION

It don't seem there could have been fifty; still, there were quite a few.
4. I don't guess I am able to realize the horrible side of war. I expect I would of if I had been there.
5. The colt kind of stayed close to it's mother, thinking it would find safety with her like it used to could. Horses are not very different than humans.

EXERCISE IN DICTION

A. Wordiness

Strike out all that is superfluous, and make the following sentences simple and exact.

1. For hunting ducks the duck hunter should have a good lot of equipment.
2. In impressing anything upon the memory one of the best ways to impress it is to write it down.
3. There was a herd of buffaloes which might have been seen grazing near the river.
4. The upstairs part of the house was what impressed me most.
5. In my opinion, I think that *The Virginian* is a very interesting book.
6. He had a fountain pen that he carried around with him to write with.
7. The vaccination didn't take, and since it didn't, he had it repeated again.
8. I am always making continuous efforts to improve my voice all the time.
9. He necessarily would have to wait for positively a whole hour.
10. We are filled with emotions of pride in the glorious flag of our country.
11. Parolles is a follower of Count Bertram, and as such is thought of by him as being a loyal and ardent one.

DICTION

12. The queen of the night arose in her splendor and began to take up her regal procession through the nocturnal sky.
13. Those who are confronted by necessity refuse to acknowledge any law whatsoever.
14. Another thing in regard to the newspapers is that they go into detail to a great extent and present small facts so that they are after all a kind of a nuisance to read.
15. I am very fond of sitting in this chair. It is a chair I like to sit in because it suits me.
16. It was the unanimous opinion of all that for admission to this class students should be required to complete beforehand certain prerequisite courses.
17. In the task which I am now trying to do, that is, to write a theme, the hardest part of the whole thing is to choose a subject on which to write.
18. Realizing the historical interest these circumstances would possess in future histories, he decided that he owed it to history to write an autobiography of his own life.

B. The Exact Word

Substitute, for inaccurate words and phrases, expressions which carry an exact and reasonable meaning.

1. It's funny, but they say most of our lakes are slowly drying.
2. Wallace aided greatly in opening to the world the theory of evolution.
3. The prevention of yellow fever was one of the most important advances medicine ever obtained.
4. The giving of pageants has gained for quite a number of years.
5. Quite a few troops fell in this battle, which was the most deciding of the war.
6. After perusing this magazine one conceives a broader scope of the world's progress.
7. Florida has a climate that makes many states green with envy.

DICTION

8. You want to take more pains or an accident will transpire one of these times.
9. A friend and myself set forth a great deal of exertion in trying to move the stone.
10. He acted more interested in business and baseball than he was in Elizabeth.
11. Did I understand you to say your mother is sick a good per cent of the time?
12. Do you think that the education conditions are as bad as Wells paints them in his book?
13. We had been talking along the line of earthquakes, and Gregg said he had once encountered one.
14. Blowing the fog horn is an awfully good way to avoid collisions at sea.
15. The first part in training a vocalist is to get her to place her tones correctly.
16. The best method in planting is done by marking off spaces, by which way you get the distances precise.
17. After a vacation the students are able to enter studies with regained energy.
18. Meat is not so nice, or so safe a proposition for eating, in hot climates as in cold. The attitude of the Hebrews toward hog's flesh was done partly on sanitary grounds.

C. Words Sometimes Confused in Meaning

Use the word which accurately expresses the thought.

1. You have —— [fewer, less] checkers on the board than I.
2. —— [Leave, Let] me inquire of the ticket agent.
3. Carlyle always wrote —— [as if, like] he felt angry.
4. The engineer declared the feat was not —— [practicable, practical].
5. McPherson's habits were not —— [hygienic, sanitary].
6. The hams, in the process of curing, were —— [hanged, hung] in the smokehouse.

DICTION

7. We are —— [all ready, already] for church —— [accept, except] Harry. He can come —— [later, latter].
8. He withdrew his savings account, —— [principal, principle] and interest.
9. Her manner was simpering and —— [affected, effected]. Ridicule had no —— [affect, effect] on her.
10. The pressure of population —— [lead, led] many Italians to —— [emigrate, immigrate] to America.
11. The manager is not a man of —— [principal, principle]. The company has failed, and the stockholders are —— [apt, likely, liable] to —— [loose, lose] all their money.
12. The trip —— [learned, taught] him that the coast of Alaska has a beauty so extraordinary as hardly to be —— [credible, creditable].
13. He used the same kind of —— [stationary, stationery] for years, and signed all his letters "Yours —— [respectfully, respectively]."
14. Children who live in —— [unhygienic, unsanitary] surroundings are —— [apt, likely, liable] to —— [loose, lose] their health. Fresh air is always —— [healthful, healthy].
15. The speaker made an —— [allusion, illusion] to a common experience. To people riding on a river their boat appears to be —— [stationary, stationery]. It is another —— [instance, instants] of optical —— [allusion, illusion].

D. Colloquialism, Slang, Faulty Idiom, etc.

The diction of the following sentences is incorrect or inappropriate for written discourse. Improve the sentences.

1. He is terribly quiet, and don't enthuse over anything.
2. One member of the committee dissents to the recommendation.

DICTION

3. Among the inventions of this period there was gunpowder, which gave the knock-out blow to feudalism.
4. He had plenty clients sitting in the waiting-room, and one party talking with him in the office.
5. Many animals can display more feeling in their eyes than humans.
6. He took exceptions against their playing the phonograph so much when he called.
7. No matter how long you are gone, when you return back I shall be awful glad to see you.
8. The doctor entrusted the package with a courier.
9. The Rev. Barrows shook hands with the couple and hoped them a happy married life.
10. I picked up the comics and like to died a-laughing.
11. I'm not nowheres near ready to go over to the lab.
12. Lincoln's attitude toward slavery as a young man was different than he held in later years.
13. I liked her considerable the first time I saw her. I wish I had of known her better.
14. The biggest part of men forget what they were learned in school, and fall into a sort of a routine.
15. In our little Lizzie we shot past the bird in the swell touring car. We thought this was pretty keen.
16. If the boatswain would of throwed the harpoon quicker, it would of been good-night for the whale.
17. We didn't try to snag the freight like we intended.
18. Ain't it funny that there's nowheres a pair of young humans like to go on warm spring days so well as a graveyard?

SPELLING

No one is able to spell all unusual words on demand. But every one must spell correctly even unusual words in formal writing. The writer has time or must take time to consult a dictionary. The best dictionaries are *Webster's New International Dictionary,* the *New Standard Dictionary* (less conservative than Webster's), the *Century Dictionary and Cyclopedia* (Volume 11 of the *Century* is the best place to look for proper names), and *Murray's New English Dictionary* (very thorough, each word being illustrated with numerous quotations to show historical development). An abridged edition of one of these (the price is one to three dollars) should be accessible to each student who cannot buy the larger volumes. The best are: *Webster's Collegiate Dictionary, Webster's Secondary School Dictionary, Funk and Wagnalls Desk Standard Dictionary,* and the *Oxford Concise Dictionary.*

But the student will be spared constant recourse to the dictionary, and will save himself much time and many humiliations, if he will employ the rules and principles which follow.

Recording Errors

70. Keep a list of all the words you misspell, copying them several times in correct form. Concentrate your effort upon a few words at a time—upon those words which you yourself actually misspell. The list will be shorter than you think. It may comprise not more

SPELLING

than twenty or thirty words. Unless you are extraordinarily deficient, it will certainly not comprise more than a hundred or a hundred and fifty. Find where your weakness lies; then master it. You can accomplish the difficult part of the task in a single afternoon. An occasional review, and constant care when you write, will make your mastery permanent.

After this, and only after this, begin slowly to learn the spelling of words which you do not yourself use often, but which are a desirable equipment for all educated men. See the list under 79. *Concentrate your efforts upon a few words at a time.* It is better to know a few exactly than a large number hazily. Form the mental habit of being always right with a small group of words, and extend this group gradually.

Exercise:

Prepare for your instructor a corrected list of words which you have misspelled in your papers to the present time.

Pronouncing Accurately

Avoid slovenly pronunciation. Careful articulation makes for correctness in spelling.

Watch the vowels of unaccented syllables; give them distinct (not exaggerated) utterance, at least until you are familiar with the spelling. Examples: *separate, opportunity, everybody, sophomore, divine.*

Sound accurately all the consonants between syllables, and do not sound a single consonant twice. Examples: *candidate, government, surprise* (not

SPELLING

> *supprise*), *omission* (compare *occasion*), *defer* (compare *differ*).
>
> Sound the *g* in final *-ing*. Examples: *eating, running*.
>
> Pronounce the *-al* of adverbs derived from adjectives in *-ic* or *-al*. Examples: *tragically, occasionally, generally, ungrammatically*.
>
> Do not transpose letters; place each letter where it belongs. Examples: *perspiration* (not *prespiration*), *tragedy* (not *tradegy*).

Note.—The principle of phonetic spelling as stated above applies to many words, but by no means to all. The Simplified Spelling Board would extend this principle by changing the spelling of words to correspond with their actual sounds. It recommends such forms as *tho, thru, enuf, quartet, catalog, program*. If the student employs these forms, he must use them consistently. Many writers oppose simplified spelling; many advocate it; many compromise. Others desire to supplant our present alphabet with one more nearly phonetic, and prefer, until this fundamental reform takes place, to preserve our present spelling as it is.

Exercise:

Copy the following words slowly, pronouncing the syllables as you write: *accidentally, accommodate, accurately, artistically, athletics* (not *atheletics*), *boundary, candidate, cavalry, commission, curiosity, defer, definite, description, despair, different, dining room, dinned, disappoint, divide, divine, emphatically, eighth, everybody, February, finally, goddess, government, hundred, hurrying, instinct,*

SPELLING

laboratory, library, lightning, might have (not *might of*), *naturally, necessary, occasionally, omission, opinion, opportunity, optimist, partner, perform, perhaps, perspiration, prescription, primitive, privilege, probably, quantity, really, recognize, recommend, reverence, separate, should have* (not *should of*), *sophomore, strictly, superintendent, surprise, temperance, tragedy, usually, whether.*

Logical Kinship in Words

Get help in spelling a difficult word by thinking of related words. To think of *ridiculous* will prevent your writing *a* for the second *i* of *ridicule;* to think of *ridicule* will prevent your writing *rediculous*. To think of *prepare* will prevent your writing *preperation;* to think of *preparation* will forestall *preparitory*. To think of *busy* will save you from the monstrosity *buisness*. To think of the prefixes *re-* (meaning *again*) and *dis-* (meaning *not*), and the verbs *commend* and *appoint*, will prevent your writing *recommend* or *disappoint* with a double *c* or *s*.

Note.—The relationship between words is not always a safe guide to spelling. Observe *four, forty; nine, ninth; maintain, maintenance; please, pleasant; speak, speech; prevail, prevalent*. Do not confuse the following prefixes, which have no logical connection:

ante- (before)   *anti-* (against, opposite)
de- (from, about)   *dis-* (apart, away, not)
per- (through, entirely) *pre-* (before)

SPELLING

Exercise:

1. Write the nouns corresponding to the following verbs: *prepare, allude, govern, represent.*
2. Write the adjectives corresponding to the following nouns and the nouns corresponding to the following adjectives: *desperation, ridiculous, miraculous, grammatical, arithmetical, busy, academy, origin.*
3. Write the adverbs corresponding to the following adjectives: *real, sure, actual, hurried, accidental, incidental, grammatical.*
4. Copy the following pairs of related words or related forms of words: *labor, laboratory; debate, debater; base, based; deal, dealt; chose, chosen; mean, meant.*
5. Write each of the following words with a hyphen between the prefix and the body of the word: *describe, description, disappoint, disappear, disease, dissatisfy, dissever, permit, perspire, prescription, preconceive, recommend, recollect, reconsider, antedate, antecedent, anticlimax, antitoxin.*

Superficial Resemblances between Words

73. Guard against misspelling a word because it bears a superficial resemblance, in sound or appearance, to some other word. Most of the words in the following list have no logical connection; the resemblance is one of form only (*angel, angle*). But a few words are included which are different in spelling in spite of a logical relation (*breath, breathe*).

accept (to receive)
except (to exclude, with exclusion of)
advice (noun)
advise (verb)
affect (to influence in part)
effect (to bring to pass totally)

allusion (a reference)
illusion (a deceiving appearance
all right
almost
already
altogether
always

SPELLING

alley (a back street)
ally (a confederate)

altar (a structure used in worship)
alter (to make otherwise)

angel (a celestial being)
angle (the meeting place of two lines)

baring (making bare)
barring (obstructing)
bearing (carrying)

born (brought into being)
borne (carried)

breath (noun)
breathe (verb)

capital (a city)
capitol (a building)

canvas (a cloth)
canvass (to solicit)

clothes (garments)
cloths (pieces of cloth)

coarse (not fine)
course (route, method of behavior)

conscious (aware)
conscience (an inner moral sense)

dairy
diary

device (noun)
devise (verb)

desert (a barren country)
dessert (food)

dining-room
dinning

disappear
disappoint

disavowal
dissatisfaction
dissimilar
dissipate
dissuade

decent (adjective)
descent (downward slope or motion)
dissent (a disagreement)

dual (adjective)
duel (noun)

formally (in a formal way)
formerly (in time past)

forth
forty
four
fourth

freshman
freshmen (not used as adjective)

gambling (wagering money on games of chance)
gamboling (frisking or leaping with joy)

guard
regard

SPELLING

hear
here

hinder
hindrance

holly (a tree)
holy (hallowed, sacred)
wholly (altogether)

hoping (from *hope*)
hopping

instance (an example)
instants (periods of time)

isle (an island)
aisle (a narrow passage)

its (possessive pronoun)
it's (contraction of *it is*)

Johnson, Samuel
Jonson, Ben

later (comparative of *late*)
latter (the second)

lead (present tense)
led (past tense)

lessen (verb)
lesson (noun)

liable (expresses responsibility
  or disagreeable probability)
likely (expresses probability)

loose (free, not bound)
lose (to suffer the loss of)

maintain
maintenance

nineteenth
ninetieth

ninety
ninth

past (adjective, adverb, preposition)
passed (verb, past tense)

peace (a state of calm)
piece (a fragment)

perceive
perform
persevere
persuade
purchase
pursue

personal (private, individual)
personnel (the body of persons
  engaged in some activity)

Philippines
Filipino

plain (clear; adjective)
plain (flat region; noun)
plane (flat; adjective)
plane (geometrical term; noun)

planed (past tense of *plane*)
planned (past tense of *plan*)

pleasant
please

precede
proceed ⎫
succeed ⎬ these three are the "double *e* group"
exceed   ⎭
concede
intercede
recede
supersede

SPELLING

pre cé dence (act or right of preceding)
préc e dents (things said or done before, now used as authority or model)

presence (state of being present)
presents (gifts)

prevail
prevalent

principal (chief, leading, the leading official of a school, a sum of money)
principle (a general truth)

quiet (still)
quite (completely)

rain
reign (rule of a monarch)
rein (part of a harness)

respectfully ("Yours respectfully")
respectively (in a way proper to each—should never be used to close a letter)

right
rite (ceremony)
write

shone (past tense of *shine*)
shown (part participle of *show*)

seize
siege

sight (view, spectacle)
site (situation, a plot of ground reserved for some use)
cite (to bring forward as evidence)

speak
speech

Spencer, Herbert (scientist)
Spenser, Edmund (poet)

stationary (not moving)
stationery (writing materials)

statue (a sculptured likeness)
stature (height, figure)
statute (a law)

steal (to take by theft)
steel (a variety of iron)

than
then

their (belonging to them)
there (in that place)
they're (they are)

therefor (to that end, for that thing)
therefore (for that reason)

till
until

to
too
two

track (an imprint, or a road)
tract (an area of land)
tract (a treatise on religion)

SPELLING

village
villain

wandering
wondering

weak (not strong)
week (seven days)

weather
whether

whole (entire)
hole (an opening)

who's (who is)
whose (the possessive of *who*)

your (indicates possession)
you're (contraction of *you are*)

Exercise:

1. Then —— [to, too, two], he wished to take the —— [coarse, course] in electricity, if he could —— [device, devise] means of so doing.
2. —— [Their, There, They're] are many reasons why we should not —— [loose, lose] control now. I shall —— [sight, site, cite] some of them.
3. The sun —— [shone, shown] —— [weak, week] and drooping, as it had a perfect —— [right, rite, write] to do.
4. The usher —— [lead, led] the visitors slowly down the —— [aisle, isle] to the —— [altar, alter]. A dim light came from the candles —— [born, borne] by boys.
5. —— [Your, You're] fortunate in having a new suit of —— [clothes, cloths]. —— [Its, It's] more than I can afford. —— [Their, There, They're] —— [to, too, two] expensive.

Words in *ei* or *ie*

74.

Write *i* before *e*
When sounded as *ee*
Except after *c*.

Examples: *believe, grief, chief;* but *receive, deceive, ceiling.*

Exceptions: *Neither financier seized either species of weird leisure.* (Also a few uncommon words, like *seignior, inveigle, plebeian.*)

SPELLING

Rules based on a key-word, lice, Alice, Celia (*i* follows *l* and *e* follows *c*) apply after two consonants only, and do not help one to spell a word like *grief*. Rule 74 applies after all consonants.

Note.—The words in which the sound is *ee* are the words really difficult to spell. When the sound is any other than *ee* (especially when it is *a*), *i* usually follows *e*. Examples: *veil, weigh, freight, neighbor, height, sleight, heir, heifer, counterfeit, foreign,* etc.

Exceptions: *ancient, friend, sieve, mischief, fiery, tries,* etc.

Exercise:

Write the following words, supplying *ei* or *ie:* th—f, —ther, s—ze, rei—f, n—ce, fr—ght, r—n, w—ld, n—ghbor, s—ge, n—ther, ach—ve, bel—f, w—rd, undec—ve, rec—pt, br—f, c—ling, sl—gh, l—sure, gr—f, f—nd, y—ld, perc—ve, conc—ve, p—rce, ap—ce.

Doubling a Final Consonant

5. **Monosyllables and words accented on the final syllable, if they end in one consonant preceded by a single vowel, double the consonant before a suffix beginning with a vowel.**

   Examples: (a) Words derived from monosyllables: *plan-ned, clan-nish, get-ting, hot-test, bag-gage.* (b) Words derived from words accented on the final syllable: *begin-ning, repel-lent, unregret-ted.*

   Note 1.—There are four distinct steps in the application of this rule. (1) The primary word must be found.

SPELLING

To decide whether *begging* contains two *g's,* we must first think of *beg.* (2) The primary word must be a monosyllable or a word accented on the final syllable. *Hit* and *allot* meet this test; *open* does not. *Deferred* and *differed, preferred* and *proffered, committed* (or *committee*) and *prohibited* double or refrain from doubling the final consonant of the primary word according to the position of the accent. The seeming discrepancy between *preferred* and *preferable,* between *conferred* and *conference,* is due to a shifting of the accent to the first syllable in the case of *preferable* and *conference.* (3) The primary word must end in one consonant. *Trace, oppose, interfere, help, reach,* and *perform* fail to meet this test, and therefore in derivatives do not double the last consonant. *Assurance* has one *r,* as it should have; *occurrence* has two *r's,* as it should have. (4) The final consonant of the primary word must be preceded by a single vowel. This principle excludes the extra consonant from *needy, daubed,* and *proceeding,* and gives it to *running.*

Note 2.—After *q, u* has the force of *w.* Hence *quitting, quizzes, squatter, acquitted, equipped,* and similar words are not really exceptions to the rule.

Exercise:

1. Write the present participle (in *-ing*) of *din* (not *dine*), *begin, sin* (compare *shine*), *stop, prefer, rob, drop, occur, omit, swim, get, commit.*
2. Write the past tense (in *-ed*) of *plan* (not *plane*), *star* (compare *stare*), *stop* (compare *slope*), *lop* (not *lope*), *hop* (not *hope*), *fit, benefit, occur* (compare *cure*), *offer, confer, bat* (compare *abate*).

SPELLING

Final e before a Suffix Beginning with a Vowel

6. **Words that end in silent *e* usually drop the *e* in derivatives or before a suffix beginning with a vowel.**

   Examples: *bride, bridal; guide, guidance; please, pleasure; fleece, fleecy; force, forcible; argue, arguing; arrive, arrival; conceive, conceivable; college, collegiate; write, writing; use, using; change, changing; judge, judging; believe, believing.*

   Note 1.—Of the exceptions some retain the *e* to prevent confusion with other words. Exceptions: *dyeing, singeing, mileage, acreage, hoeing, shoeing, agreeing, eyeing.* The exceptions cause comparatively little trouble. One rarely sees *hoing* or *shoing;* he often sees *hopeing* and *inviteing.*

   Note 2.—After *c* or *g* and before a suffix beginning with *a* or *o* the *e* is retained. The purpose of this retention is to preserve the soft sound of the *c* or *g*. (Observe that *c* and *g* have the hard sound in *cable, gable, cold, go.*)

   Examples: *peaceable, changeable, noticeable, serviceable, outrageous, courageous, advantageous.*

Exercise:
1. Write the present participle of the following words: *use, love, change, judge, shake, hope, shine, have, seize, slope, strike, dine, come, place, argue, achieve, emerge, arrange, abide, oblige, subdue.*
2. Write the present participle of the following words: *singe, tinge, dye, agree, eye.*
3. Write the *-ous* or *-able* form of the following words: *trace,*

SPELLING

love, blame, move, conceive, courage, service, advantage, umbrage.
4. Write the adjectives which correspond to the following nouns: *force, sphere, vice, sense, fleece, college, hygiene.*
5. Write the nouns which correspond to the following verbs: *please, guide, grieve, arrive, oblige, prepare, inspire.*

Plurals

77a. **Most nouns add *s* or *es* to form the plural.** Examples: *word, words; fire, fires; negro, negroes; Eskimo, Eskimos; leaf, leaves* (*f* changes to *v* for the sake of euphony); *knife, knives.*

b. **Nouns ending in *y* preceded by a consonant (or by *u* as *w*) change the *y* to *i* and add *es* to form the plural.** Examples: *sky, skies; lady, ladies; colloquy, colloquies; soliloquy, soliloquies.*

Other nouns ending in *y* form the plural in the usual way. Examples: *day, days; boy, boys; monkey, monkeys; valley, valleys.*

c. **Compound nouns usually form the plural by adding *s* or *es* to the principal word.** Examples: *sons-in-law, passers-by;* but *stand-bys.*

d. **Letters, signs, and sometimes figures, add 's to form the plural.** Examples: Cross your t's and dot your i's; ?'s; $'s; 3's or 3s.

e. **A few nouns adhere to old declensions.** Examples: *ox, oxen; child, children; goose, geese; foot, feet; mouse, mice; man, men; woman, women; sheep, sheep; deer, deer; swine, swine.*

SPELLING

f. Words adopted from foreign languages sometimes retain the foreign plural. Examples: *alumnus, alumni; alumna, alumnæ; fungus, fungi; focus, foci; radius, radii; datum, data; medium, media; phenomenon, phenomena; stratum, strata; analysis, analyses; antithesis, antitheses; basis, bases; crisis, crises; oasis, oases; hypothesis, hypotheses, parenthesis, parentheses; thesis, theses; beau, beaux; tableau, tableaux; Mr., Messrs. (Messieurs); Mrs., Mmes. (Mesdames).*

Exercise:

Write the singular and plural of the following words: *day, sky, lady, wife, leaf, loaf, negro, potato, tomato, pass, glass, boat, beet, flash, crash, bead, box, passenger, messenger, son-in-law, Smith, Jones, jack-o'-lantern, hanger-on, stratum, datum, phenomenon, crisis, basis, thesis, analysis.*

Compounds

78a. Use a hyphen between two or more words which serve as a single adjective before a noun: *iron-bound bucket, well-kept lawn, twelve-inch main, normal-school teacher, up-to-date methods, twentieth-century ideas, devil-may-care expression, a twenty-dollar-a-week clerk.*

But when the words follow the noun, the hyphen is omitted. *The lawn is well kept. Methods up to date in every way.*

Also adverbs ending in *-ly* are not ordinarily made into compound modifiers: *nicely kept lawn, securely guarded treasure.*

b. Use a hyphen between members of a compound noun when the second member is a preposition, or when

78
SPELLING

the writing of two nouns solid or separately might confuse the meaning: *runner-up, kick-off, letting-down of effort, son-in-law, jack-o'-lantern, Pedro was a bull-fighter, a woman-hater, Did you ever see a shoe-polish like this?*

c. Use a hyphen in compound numbers from twenty-one to ninety-nine, and in fractions according to the following examples:

Twenty-three, eighty-nine; but *one hundred and one.*
Twenty-third, one-hundred-and-first man.
Three-fourths, four and two-thirds, thirty-hundredths, thirty-one hundredths.

But omit the hyphen in simple fractions when loosely used: *Three quarters of my life are spent. One third of his fortune.*

d. A hyphen is not used in the following common words: *airship, altogether, anybody, baseball, basketball, everybody, football, goodby, herself, handbook, himself, inasmuch, itself, midnight, myself, nevertheless, nobody, nothing* (but *no one*), *nowadays, railroad, themselves, together, typewritten, wherever, without, workshop, yourself, newspaper, sunset.*

e. For words that do not come within the scope of rules, consult an up-to-date dictionary. Compounds tend, with the passing of time, to grow together. Once men wrote *steam boat,* later *steam-boat,* and finally *steamboat.* New-coined words are usually hyphenated; old words are often written solid. The degree of intimacy between the parts of a compound word affects usage;

SPELLING

thus we write *sun-motor,* but *sunbeam; birth-rate,* but *birthday; cooling-room,* but *bedroom; non-conductor,* but *nonsense.* The ease with which a vowel blends with the consonant of a syllable adjoining it affects usage; thus *self-evident,* but *selfsame; non-existent,* but *nondescript; un-American,* but *unwise.* Many compounds, however, are still uncontrolled by usage; whether they should be written as two words or one, whether with or without the hyphen, the dictionaries themselves do not agree.

Exercise:

Copy the following expressions, inserting hyphens where they are necessary: *a business like step, a death like stillness, normal school teacher, a twenty dollar a week clerk, a touch me not expression, two dollar gloves, faces much wrinkled, jumping off place, two headed calves, night blooming lily, a vigorous wind up, a coat out at elbows, extravagantly dressed fellows, heavier than air craft, altogether without railroads, twenty five feet of one inch pipe, fortunate president elect, prospective son in law, seventy five dollar bills with four fifths as many more make one hundred and thirty five dollars, an I'm ready let's go expression, a lady in waiting, a self confessed tax dodger, a left handed monkey wrench, one man government, a snapper up of trifles, the wished for spelling bee, a Congressman at large.*

SPELLING LIST

The English language comprises about 450,000 words. Of these a student uses about 4,000 (although he may understand more than twice that number when he encounters them in sentences). Of these, in turn, not more than four or five hundred are frequently mis-

SPELLING

spelled. The following list includes nearly all of the words which give serious trouble. Certain American colleges using this list require of freshmen an accuracy of ninety per cent.

absurd	annual	**benefited**	compelled
academy	anxiety	biscuit	competent
accept	apparatus	boundaries	concede
accidentally	**appearance**	brilliant	conceivable
accommodate	appropriate	**Britain**	**conferred**
accumulate	arctic	**Britannica**	conquer
accustom	**argument**	buoyant	conqueror
acquainted	**arising**	bureau	conscience
acquitted	**arithmetic**	**business**	conscientious
across	arrange	**busy**	considered
addressed	arrival		continuous
adviser	ascend	calendar	control
aeroplane	asks	**candidate**	**controlled**
affects	**athletic**	can't	coöperate
aggravate	audience	cemetery	country
alley	auxiliary	**certain**	**course**
allotted	awkward	**changeable**	**courteous**
all right		changing	courtesy
ally	balance	characteristic	cruelty
already	barbarous	chauffeur	cylinder
altar	baring	**choose**	
alter	barring	chose	**dealt**
altogether	baseball	chosen	debater
alumnus	**based**	**clothes**	deceitful
always	bearing	**coarse**	decide
amateur	**becoming**	column	decision
among	before	**coming**	deferred
analogous	beggar	commission	**definite**
analysis	**begging**	**committee**	derived
angel	**beginning**	comparative	descend
angle	**believing**	**compel**	**describe**

170

SPELLING

description
despair
desperate
destroy
device
devise
dictionary
difference
digging
dilemma
dining room
dinning
disappear
disappoint
disavowal
discipline
disease
dissatisfied
dissipate
distinction
distribute
divide
divine
doctor
don't
dormitories
drudgery
dying

ecstasy
effects
eighth
eliminate
embarrass
eminent
encouraging

enemy
equipped
especially
etc.
everybody
exaggerate
exceed
excellent
except
exceptional
exhaust
exhilarate
existence
expense
experience
explanation

familiar
fascinate
February
fiery
fifth
finally
financier
forfeit
formally
formerly
forth
forty
fourth
frantically
fraternity
freshman
(adj.)
friend
fulfil
furniture

gallant
gambling
generally
goddess
government
governor
grammar
grandeur
grievous
guard
guess
guidance

harass
haul
having
height
hesitancy
holy
hoping
huge
humorous
hundredths
hurriedly
hygienic

imaginary
imitative
immediately
immigration
imminent
impromptu
incidentally
incidents
incredulous
independence
indispensable

induce
influence
infinite
instance
instant
intellectual
intelligence
intentionally
intercede
invitation
irresistible
its
it's
itself

judgment

knowledge

laboratory
ladies
laid
later
latter
lead
led
liable
library
lightning
likely
literature
loneliness
loose
lose
losing
lying

SPELLING

maintain
maintenance
manual
manufacturer
many
marriage
Massachusetts
material
mathematics
mattress
meant
messenger
miniature
minutes
mischievous
Mississippi
misspelled
momentous
month
murmur
muscle
mysterious

necessary
negroes
neither
nickel
nineteenth
ninetieth
ninety
ninth
noticeable
nowadays

oblige
obstacle

occasion
occasionally
occur
occurred
occurrence
occurring
o'clock
officers
omission
omitted
opinion
opportunity
optimistic
original
outrageous
overrun

paid
pantomime
parallel
parliament
particularly
partner
pastime
peaceable
perceive
perception
peremptory
perform
perhaps
permissible
perseverance
pérsonal
personnél
perspiration
persuade
pertain

pervade
physical
picnic
picnicking
planned
pleasant
politician
politics
possession
possible
practically
prairie
precede
precédence
précedents
preference
preferred
prejudice
preparation
primitive
principal
principle
prisoner
privilege
probably
proceed
prodigy
profession
professor
proffered
prohibition
promissory
prove
purchase
pursue
putting

quantity
quiet
quite
quizzes
rapid
ready
really
recede
receive
recognize
recommend
reference
referred
regard
region
religion
religious
repetition
replies
representative
restaurant
rheumatism
ridiculous

sacrilegious
safety
sandwich
schedule
science
scream
screech
seems
seize
sense
sentence
separate
sergeant

SPELLING

several	**stories**	track	weak
shiftless	stretch	tract	wear
shining	**strictly**	**tragedy**	weather
shone	succeeds	tranquillity	**Wednesday**
shown	successful	transferred	week
shriek	summarize	translate	**weird**
siege	**superintendent**	treacherous	welfare
similar	supersede	treasurer	where
since	**sure**	**tries**	wherever
smooth	**surprise**	**trouble**	**whether**
soliloquy	syllable	**truly**	which
sophomore	symmetrical	**Tuesday**	whole
speak		two	**wholly**
specimen	**temperament**	typical	**who's**
speech	**tendency**	tyranny	whose
statement	than		wintry
stationary	**their**	universally	wiry
stationery	there	**until**	within
statue	therefore	**using**	without
stature	**they're**	**usually**	**women**
statute	thorough		world
steal	thousandths	vacancy	**writing**
steel	till	vengeance	written
stops	to	vigilance	
stopped	**together**	**village**	your
stopping	**too**	**villain**	**you're**

Note 1.—The following words have more than one **correct** form, the one given here being preferred.

abridgment	check	gaiety	meter
acknowledgment	criticize	gild	mold
analyze	develop	gipsy	mustache
ax	development	glamor	odor
boulder	dulness	goodby	program
caliber	endorse	gray	prolog
catalog	envelop	inquire	skilful
center	esthetic	medieval	theater

SPELLING

Note 2.—In a few groups of words American spelling and English spelling differ. American spelling gives preference to *favor, honor, labor, rumor;* English spelling gives preference to *favour, honour, labour, rumour.* American spelling gives preference to *civilize, apprize; defense, pretense; traveler, woolen;* etc. English spelling gives preference to *civilise, apprise; defence, pretence; traveller, woollen;* etc.

MISCELLANEOUS

Manuscript

a. Titles. Center a title on the page. Capitalize important words. It is unnecessary to place a period after a title, but a question mark or exclamation point should be used when one is appropriate. Do not underscore the title, or unnecessarily place it in quotation marks. Leave a blank line under the title, before beginning the body of the writing.

Spacing. Careful spacing is as necessary as punctuation. Place writing on a page as you would frame a picture, crowding it toward neither the top nor the bottom. Leave liberal margins. Write verse as verse; do not give it equal indention or length of line with prose. Connect all the letters of a word. Leave a space after a word, and a double space after a sentence. Leave room between successive lines, and do not let the loops of letters run into the lines above or below.

Handwriting. Write a clear, legible hand. Form *a, o, u, n, e, i* properly. Write out *and* horizontally. Avoid unnecessary flourishes in capitals, and curlicues at the end of words. Dot your *i's* and cross your *t's;* not with circles or long eccentric strokes, but simply and accurately. Let your originality express itself not in ornate penmanship, or unusual stationery, or literary affectations, but in the force and keenness of your ideas.

CAPITALS

Capitals

81a. Begin with a capital a sentence, a line of poetry, or a quoted sentence. But if only a fragment of a sentence is quoted, the capital should be omitted.

> Right: He said, "The time has come."
> Right: The question is, Shall the bill pass?
> Right: They said they would "not take no for an answer."
> Right: "The good die first,
> And they whose hearts are dry as summer dust
> Burn to the socket."—Wordsworth.

b. Begin proper names, and all important words used as or in proper names, with capitals. Words not so used should not begin with capitals.

> Right: Mr. George K. Rogers, the Principal of the Urbana High School, a college president, the President of the Senior Class, a senior, the Second Corps of the Army of Northern Virginia, three battalions of infantry, the Fourth of July, on the tenth of June, the House of Representatives, an assembly of delegates, a Presbyterian church, the separation of church and state, the Baptist Church, the Society for the Prevention of Cruelty to Animals, a creek known as Black Oak Creek, the Republican Party, a party that advocates high tariff, Rocky Mountains, The Bible, God, The Christian Era, Wednesday, in the summer, living in the South, turning south after taking a few steps to the east, one morning, O dark-haired Evening! italic type, watt, pasteurize, herculean effort.

c. Begin an adjective which designates a language or a race with a capital.

> Right: A Norwegian peasant, Indian arrowheads, English literature, the study of French.

CAPITALS

- In the titles of books or themes capitalize the first word and all other important words. Prepositions, conjunctions, and articles are usually not important.

    Right: *The English Novel in the Time of Scott, War and Peace, Travels with a Donkey, When I Slept under the Stars.*

- Miscellaneous uses. Capitalize the pronoun *I*, the interjection *O*, titles that accompany a name, and abbreviations of proper names.

    Right: Battery F, 150 F. A.; Mobile, Ala.; Dr. Stebbins.

Exercise:

1. the return of the native by thomas hardy opens with a description of egdon heath.
2. on christmas day, or some day in december not long before christmas, the pastor of the congregational church preaches a sermon on charity.
3. near richmond, virginia, we saw a fine old house with doric columns. the house was built of brick shipped over from england in the eighteenth century—before the revolutionary war.
4. today we find the grandsons of the men who developed the ohio river valley and later the land west of the mississippi river going into canada and assisting in the development of the province of alberta and the northwestern territory.
5. in the middle ages, little was known of the land beyond southern europe, northern africa, and western asia. the crusades extended geographical knowledge. in 1295 marco polo crossed asia and visited china. in the fifteenth century the portuguese discovered a new route to the east. in turn, diaz rounded the cape of good hope, columbus discovered america, the cabots explored the northern part of america, and vespucius made a voyage to south america.

Italics

In manuscript, a horizontal line drawn under a letter or word is a sign for the printer to use italic type.

82a. Quoted titles of books, periodicals, and manuscripts are usually italicized.

> Right: I admire Shakespeare's *Hamlet*. [The italics make the reader know that the writer means *Hamlet* the play, not Hamlet the man.]
>
> Right: John Galsworthy's novel, *The Patrician,* appeared in serial form in the *Atlantic Monthly*.

Note 1.—When the title of a book begins with an article (*a, an,* or *the*), the article is italicized. But *the* before the title of a periodical is usually not italicized.

Note 2.—It is correct, but not the best practice, to indicate the titles of books by quotation marks. The best method is to use italics for the title of a book, and quotation marks for chapters or subdivisions of the same book. Example: See *Encyclopedia Britannica,* Vol. II, p. 427, "Modern Architecture."

b. Words from a foreign language, unless they have been anglicized by frequent use, are italicized.

> Right: A great noise announced the coming of the *enfant terrible*.
>
> Right: A play always begins *in medias res*.

c. The names of ships are usually italicized.

> Right: The *Saxonia* will sail at four o'clock.

ABBREVIATIONS

- Words taken out of their context and made the subject of discussion are italicized or placed in quotation marks.

    Right: *So* is a word faded and colorless from constant use.
    Right: The *t* in the word *often* is not pronounced.

- A word or passage requiring great emphasis is italicized. This device should not be used to excess. The proper way to secure emphasis is to have good ideas, and to use emphatic sentence structure in expressing them.

Exercise:

1. Is there one l in traveler, or are there two?
2. I may say, entre nous, that he did not take passage on the Aquitania.
3. Since the war there has been renewed interest in Tolstoi's novel, War and Peace.
4. Fault, let, love, and vantage are technical terms in tennis that you should learn at the outset.
5. When I first visited London, the Englishman's Thank you's seemed to me amazingly numerous. I asked a man riding in the Underground if I might see his copy of the Spectator. He replied, "By all means. Thank you." Often the Englishman accents the second word with a rising inflection, thus, "Thank you!" Countless times I heard on the street the same cheerful phrase. "What time is it, please?"—"Half after six; thank you!" . . . "How do I get to the British Museum?" —"Take the bus marked thirteen;—thank you!"

Abbreviations

- In ordinary writing avoid abbreviations. The following, however, are always correct: Mr., Messrs.,

ABBREVIATIONS

Dr., or **St.** (Saint), before proper names; **B. C.** or **A. D.**, when necessary to avoid confusion, after a date; and **No.** or **$** when followed by numerals.

In ordinary writing spell out

All titles, except those listed above.
Names of months, states, countries.
Christian names, unless initials are used instead.
Names of weights and measures, except in statistics.
Street, Avenue, Road, Railroad, Park, Fort, Mountain, Company, Brothers, Manufacturing, etc.

In ordinary writing, instead of & write *and;* for *viz.* write *namely;* for *i. e.*, write *that is;* for *e. g.* write *for example;* for *a. m.* and *p. m.* write *in the morning, this afternoon, tomorrow evening, Saturday night.* Do not use *etc.* (*et cetera*) when it can be avoided. Never place the word *and* before the sign *etc.* The Latin *et* means *and.*

b. In business correspondence, technical writing, tabulations, footnotes, and bibliographies, or wherever brevity is essential, other abbreviations may be used. Even here, short words should not be abbreviated: Alaska, Hawaii, Idaho, Iowa, Maine, Ohio, Samoa, Utah, March, April, May, June, July.

Exercise:
1. Yrs. rec'd. and we have directed our Mr. Huxtable to call on you before the end of the mo.
2. My bro. and I went over the co.'s records, etc.
3. The usual groceries, dry goods stores, drug stores, and etc., are found on Main Street.

NUMBERS

4. Geo. Washington, Thos. Jefferson, and Robt. E. Lee were born in Va.
5. The av. amt. of time put in daily by the employees of the acc't. dept. is 8 hrs. On Sat. p.m. no work is done in the bldg.

Numbers

a. It is customary to use figures for dates, for the street numbers in addresses, for reference to the pages of a book, and for statistics.

Right: June 16, 1922. 804 Chalmers Street. See Chapter 4, especially page 79.

Note.—It is desirable not to write *st, nd,* or *th* after the day of the month if the year is designated also. Right: March 3, 1922 (not March 3rd, 1922).

Figures are used for numbers which cannot be expressed in a few words. The dollar sign and figures are used with complicated sums of money.

Right: The farm comprised 3,260 acres. The population of Kansas City, Missouri, was 324,410 in 1920. He earned $437 while attending school. The cost of the improvement was $1,940.25.

In other instances than those specified in *a* and *b*, numbers as a rule should be written out. (This rule applies to numbers and to sums of money which can be expressed in a few words, to sums of money less than one dollar, and to ages and time of day.)

Right: The box weighs two hundred pounds. Xerxes had an army of three million men. I enclose seventy-

SYLLABICATION

five cents. He owed twelve hundred dollars. Grandfather Toland is eighty-seven years old. The train is due at a quarter past three.

Exercise:
1. We bought 1 quart of certified milk for $0.30. I think I met 1,000 people in those six blocks.
2. You can ride 30 miles on the street car for 20 cents. This bullet had been traveling 2,000 feet per second for 5 seconds.
3. The moon has a diameter of 2,162 miles, is 238,840 miles from the earth, and completes its orbit in twenty-seven and one-third days.
4. The government survey was made in nineteen hundred and thirteen, and comprises a quadrangle of nine hundred and thirty square miles. The map of this area is about 16½ by 20 inches in size, being drawn on a scale of 2 miles to the inch.
5. I enclose eighty-five dollars, for which please ship me 1 thousand board feet of 1 inch finishing lumber, 1st quality, as follows:

      36 pcs. 1 x 8 —14' Oregon fir
      125 "   1 x 4 —16'   "   "

Syllabication

85a. When a word is broken at the end of a line, use a hyphen there. Do not place a hyphen at the beginning of the second line.

b. Words are divided only between syllables: *department, dis-charge, ab-surd, univer-sity, pro-fessor* (not *depa-rtment, disc-harge, abs-urd, unive-rsity, prof-essor*).

SYLLABICATION

- **Monosyllabic words are never divided:** *which, through, dipped, speak* (not *wh-ich, thr-ough, dip-ped, spe-ak*).
- **A consonant at the junction of two syllables usually goes with the second:** *recipro-cate, ordi-nance, inti-mate* (not *reciproc-ate, ordin-ance, intim-ate*). Sometimes two consonants are equivalent to a single letter: *falli-ble, photo-graph* (not *fallib-le, photog-raph*).
- **Two or more consonants at the junction of syllables are themselves divided:** *en-ter-prise, com-mis-sary, in-car-nate* (not *ent-erpr-ise, comm-iss-ary, inc-arn-ate*).
- **A prefix or a suffix is usually set off from the rest of the word regardless of the rule for consonants between syllables:** *ex-empt, dis-appoint, sing-ing, pro-gress-ive*. But when a final consonant is doubled before a suffix the additional consonant goes with the suffix: *trip-ping, permit-ted, omis-sion*.
- **The best usage avoids separating one or two letters (unless in prefixes like *un* or suffixes like *ly*) from the rest of the word:** *achieve-ment, enor-mous, re-membered, dyspep-sia* (not *a-chievement, e-normous, remember-ed, dyspepsi-a*).

Exercise:

Place a hyphen between each pair of syllables in each word of more than one syllable: miscreant, rigging, struck, undergo, mystify, attribute, contribute, disappear, misspell, perspiration, infallible, entering, disaster, annually, enough, scoundrel, sloped, suppress, transgressing, implicate, retarded, occurrence, rebuttal, infraction, cough, whipped, psychology, perplexity, encroachment, curve, asbestos, twinge, vertebra, luggage, ecstasy, improvise, flagrant, buckskin, yacht, doctrine, matriculate, stealth, recollect, recommend, analysis.

Outlines

Three kinds of outlines are illustrated in this article: (a) the Topic Outline, (b) the Sentence Outline, and (c) the Paragraph Outline.

86a. A topic outline consists of headings (nouns or phrases containing nouns) which indicate the important ideas in a composition, and their relation to each other. Conform to the following model:

The Lumber Problem

Theme: The decline of our lumber supply requires that we shall take steps toward reforesting, conservation, and the use of substitutes for wood.

I The Depletion of our forests
    A Former abundance
    B Present scarcity (especially walnut, white pine, oak)

II The Causes of the depletion
    A Great demand
        1 For building
        2 For industrial expansion (ties, posts, etc.)
        3 For fuel, and other minor uses
    B Wasteful methods of forestry

III The Remedy
    A Reforestation
        1 Planting by individuals
        2 Planting by the states
        3 Extension of the present National Forest Reserves
    B The prevention of waste
        1 In fires, by insects, etc.
        2 In cutting and sawing
        3 In by-products (sawdust, odd lengths, etc.

OUTLINES

      C The use of substitutes for wood (concrete, steel, brick, stone, etc.)

b. A sentence outline is expressed in complete sentences, punctuated as in ordinary discourse. Conform to the following model:

The Lumber Problem

I The depletion of our forests is evident when one compares

    A the former abundance, with

    B the present scarcity (of walnut, white pine, and oak, especially).

II The causes of the depletion are:

    A the great demand
        1 for building,
        2 for industrial expansion (ties, posts, etc.),
        3 for fuel and other minor uses; and

    B wasteful methods of forestry.

III The remedies for the depletion are:

    A reforestation
        1 by individuals,
        2 by the states,
        3 by extension of the present National Forest Reserves;

    B the prevention of waste
        1 in fires, by insects, etc.,
        2 in cutting and sawing,
        3 in by-products (sawdust, odd lengths, etc.); and

    C the use of substitutes for wood (concrete, steel, brick, stone, etc.).

c. A paragraph outline is a series of sentences summarizing the thought of successive paragraphs in a composition. Conform to the following model:

The Disagreeable Optimist

1. The present age may be called an era of efficiency, prosperity, and optimism, since efficiency has produced prosperity, and this in turn has produced "optimism"—a word recurrent in common literature and conversation.
2. The optimist is often not natural or sincere, because his thoughts are centered on keeping up an appearance of being happy.
3. He is intrusive, for he thrusts comfort upon those who wish to mourn, and repeats irritating epigrams and poems about cheer.
4. He is undiscriminating, in that he prescribes the same remedy, "good cheer," for everybody and for every condition.
5. He is sometimes harmful, because he tells us that the world is going well, when conditions need changing, and need changing badly.

d. Mechanical details. Indent headings that are coördinate (that is, of equal value) an equal distance from the margin. One inch to the right is a good distance for successive subordinate headings. Use Roman numerals, capital letters, Arabic numerals, and small letters to indicate the comparative rank of ideas. When a heading runs over one line, use hanging indention; that is, do not allow the second line to run back to the left-hand margin, but indent it. Make the numerals and

OUTLINES

letters (*I*, *A*, etc.) stand out prominently. The title of a theme should not be given a numeral or letter.

Faulty indention:

Sources of energy which may be utilized when the coal supply is exhausted are

       I Rivers and streams, especially in mountain districts
        II The tides
        III The heat of the sun

Correct hanging indention:

Sources of energy which may be utilized when the coal supply is exhausted are

       I Rivers and streams, especially in mountain
         districts
        II The tides
        III The heat of the sun

e. Ideas parallel in thought should be expressed in parallel form. Nouns and phrases including nouns are ordinarily used.

Faulty parallelism:

Advantages of a garden:

    1 Profitable
    2 It affords good exercise
    3 Gives pleasure

Right:

Advantages of a garden:

    1 Profit
    2 Exercise
    3 Pleasure

OUTLINES

f. Avoid faulty coördination (giving two ideas equal rank, when one should be subordinated to the other) and *vice versa,* avoid faulty subordination.

Faulty coördination:

How Seeds Scatter

    I By Wind
   II Some Seeds provided with parachutes
  III Others light, and easily blown about
  IV By Water
   V By Animals

Right:

How Seeds Scatter

  I By Wind
    A Some seeds provided with parachutes
    B Others light, and easily blown about
 II By Water
III By Animals

g. Avoid detailed subordination. Especially avoid a single subheading when it can be joined to the preceding line, or omitted.

Too detailed:

  A The McClellan Orchard
    1 Situation
      a On a northern slope
    2 Nature of soil
      a Sandy
    3 Kind of fruit
      a Apple
      b Cherry

OUTLINES

Right:

>A The McClellan Orchard
>
>>1. Situation: a northern slope
>>2. Nature of soil: sandy
>>3. Kind of fruit: apple and cherry

Exercise:

1. Place in order the headings of the following outline on "Tennis as an All-Round Sport." Subordinate some of the headings to others. If necessary, change the wording, or introduce new headings.

    >A Game that Can Be Played Anywhere
    >A Game that Can Be Made either Strenuous or Easy
    >A Game that Can Be Played by Old or Young
    >A Game (Unlike Football, Golf, Rowing, etc.) Independent of Special Facilities not Likely to Be Had in Ordinary Towns
    >A Game that Can Be Played by Men or Women
    >A Game that Can Be Played by the Skilled or the Unskilled
    >One of the Most Healthful Games
    >A Game that Can Be Played by Anybody

2. Give a title to the following outline. Place the sentences in order, subordinating some to others. Introduce headings or subheadings of your own, if you find that such are necessary.

    >A dictaphone is an instrument into which one dictates letters. The instrument later reproduces the words for an operator, who types them.
    >The dictator does not have to wait until a stenographer is ready.
    >The operator may turn back a record several times if she fails to understand at first.
    >The records soon become worn and the sounds of

the words indistinct; thus a combination of poor dictator and poor operator wastes the time of both.

The dictator who so chooses may compose his letters before or after office hours without requiring the stenographer to put in extra time.

In disputes as to what the dictator said, the record furnishes the means for an accurate settlement.

If the dictator wishes to change the wording, he must say "Correction" and give the new version. If the operator does not hear the record through before beginning to type it, such corrections waste her time and the office stationery.

Many dictators are ignorant, careless, and inefficient, and their dictation is very trying to operators. In offices where large numbers do each a little dictating, some are sure to be slovenly.

Good operators are hard to procure.

The operator may do other work if the machine does not require her whole time.

Letters

The parts of a letter are the heading, the inside address, the greeting, the body, the close, and the signature. For these parts good use prescribes definite forms, which we may sometimes ignore in personal letters, but must rigidly observe in formal or business letters.

87a. The heading of a letter should give the full address of the writer and the date of writing. Do not abbreviate short words, or omit Street or Avenue.

Objectionable: # 15 Hickory, Omaha.
Right: 15 Hickory Street, Omaha, Nebraska.
Objectionable: 4/12/19; 10-28-'21; May 2nd, 1910.
Right: April 12, 1919; October 28, 1921; May 2, 1910.

LETTERS

The following headings are correct:

> 106 East Race Street,
> Red Oak, Iowa,
> August 4, 1920.

> 423 Michigan Avenue
> Chicago, Illinois
> May 20, 1922

> Prescott, Arizona, June 1, 1922.

Note.—In personal letters the heading may be transferred to the end, below the signature, at the left-hand side. But it must not be so divided that the street address will appear in one place and the town and state in another.

The "closed" form of punctuation (the use of punctuation at the ends of the lines) is best until the student learns what is correct. Afterward, the adoption of the "open" form becomes purely a matter of individual taste and not a matter of carelessness or ignorance.

b. An inside address and a greeting are required in business letters. Personal letters contain the greeting, but may omit the inside address, or may supply it at the end of the letter.

The Jeffrey Chemical Works,
   510 Marion Street,
      Norfolk, Virginia.
Gentlemen:

Mr. Joseph N. Kellogg
1411 Lake Street
Cleveland, Ohio
Dear Mr. Kellogg:

LETTERS

Secretary of Rice Institute,
    Houston, Texas.

My dear Sir:

Greetings used in business letters are:

    My dear Sir: Sir:
    My dear Madam: Sirs:
    My dear Mr. Fisher: Gentlemen:
    Dear Sir: Ladies:

Greetings used in personal letters are:

    My dear Miss Brown: Dear Mrs. Vincent,
    Dear Professor Ward: Dear Robert,
    Dear Jones,   Dear Olive,

"My dear Miss Brown" is more ceremonious than "Dear Miss Brown". As a rule, the more familiar the letter, the shorter the greeting.

A colon follows the greeting if the letter is formal or long; a comma, if the letter is familiar or in the nature of a note.

Both inside address and greeting begin at the left-hand margin. The body of the letter begins on the line below the greeting, and is indented as much as an ordinary paragraph (about an inch).

C. The body of a letter should be written in correct style.

  1. Do not omit pronouns, or write a "telegraphic style".

    Wrong: Just received yours of the 21st, and in reply would say your order has been filled and shipped.

    Right: I have your letter of March twenty-first. Your order was promptly filled and shipped.

LETTERS

2. The idea that it is immodest to use *I* is a superstition. Undue repetition of *I* is of course awkward; but entire avoidance of it is silly.
3. Use simple language. Say "your letter"; not "your kind favor", or "yours duly received", or "yours of the 21st is at hand".
4. Avoid "begging" expressions which you obviously do not mean, especially the hackneyed "beg to advise".

   Wrong: Received yours of the 3rd instant, and beg to advise we are out of stock.
   Right: We received your order of March 3. We find that we have no more dining-room chairs B 2-4-6 in stock.
   Wrong: I beg to enclose a booklet.
   Right: I enclose a booklet.
   Wrong: Permit us to say that prices have been advanced.
   Right: The prices on our goods have been advanced.

5. Avoid the formula "please find enclosed". The reader will find what is enclosed; if you use "please", let it refer to what the reader shall do with what is enclosed.

   Wrong: Enclosed please find 10 cents, for which send me Bulletin 58.
   Right: I enclose ten cents, for which please send me Bulletin 58.

6. Avoid unnecessary commercial slang: *On the job, A-1 service, O. K., your ad, popular-priced line, this party, as per schedule.*
7. Get to the important idea quickly. In applying for a position, do not beat around the bush, or say you "wish to apply" or "would apply". Begin, "I make application for . . .", "Kindly consider my application for . . .", or "I apply . . ."

LETTERS

8. Group your ideas logically. Do not scatter information. A letter applying for a position might consist of three paragraphs: Personal qualifications (age, health, education, etc.); Experience (nature of positions, dates, etc.); References (names, business or profession, exact street address). Finish one group of ideas before passing to the next.

9. Do not monotonously close all letters with a sentence beginning with a participle: *Hoping to hear from you . . . , Asking your coöperation . . . , Awaiting your further favors . . . , Trusting this will be satisfactory . . . , Wishing you . . . , Thanking you . . . .* The independent form of the verb is more emphatic (see 42); I hope to hear from you . . . , We await further orders . . . , We ask coöperation . . . .

d. The close should be consistent in tone with the greeting. It is written on a separate line, beginning near the middle of the page, and is followed by a comma. Only the first word is capitalized. Preceding expressions like "I am", "I remain", "As ever", (if they are used at all) belong in the body of the letter.

Right: I thank you for your courtesy, and remain

      Yours sincerely,
      Robert Blair

Right: I shall be grateful for any further information you can give me.

      Yours truly,
      Florence Mitchell

LETTERS

business. 87

In business letters the following forms are used:

>Yours truly,
>Very truly yours,
>Yours respectfully,

In personal letters the following are used:

>Yours truly,
>Yours sincerely,
>Sincerely yours,
>Cordially yours,

The outside address should follow one of the forms given below:

R. E. Stearns
512 Chapel Hill St.
Durham, N. C.

>Mr. Donald Kemp
>>3314 Salem Street
>>>Baltimore
>>>>Maryland

Bentley Davis
906 Park Street
Ogden, Utah

>Rogers, Mead, and Company
>2401 Eighth Avenue
>Los Angeles
>California

195

LETTERS

Note.—An abbreviation in an address is followed by a period. Punctuation is also correct, but not necessary, after every line (a period after the last line, and a comma after the others).

A married woman is ordinarily addressed thus: Mrs. George H. Turner (rather than Mrs. Grace Turner). But a title belonging to the husband should not be transferred to the wife. Wrong: Mrs. Dr. Jenkins, Mrs. Professor Ward. Right: Mrs. Jenkins, Mrs. Ward. Reverend Mr. Beecher is a correct address for a minister; not "Rev. Beecher". If a title of respect is placed before a name (Professor, Dr., Honorable), it is undesirable to place another title after the name (Secretary, M.D., Ph.D., Principal, Esq.).

f. Miscellaneous directions. Writing should be centered on the page, not crowded against the top, or against one side. Letter paper so folded that each sheet is a little book of four pages is best for personal correspondence. Both sides of such paper may be written on. The pages may be written on in any order which will be convenient to the reader. An order like that of the pages in a printed book (1, 2, 3, 4) is best.

Business letters are usually written on one side only of flat sheets 8½ by 11 inches in size. The sheet is folded once horizontally in the middle, and twice in the other direction, for insertion in the envelope.

g. A business letter should have, in general, the following form:

LETTERS

>1516 South Garrison Avenue
>Carthage, Missouri,
>May 14, 1922.

J. E. Pratt, General Superintendent,
 The Southwest Missouri Railroad Company,
  1012 North Madison Street,
   Webb City, Missouri.

Dear Sir:

I apply for a position as mechanic's assistant in the electrical department of your shops. I am nineteen years old, and in good physical condition. On June 6 I shall graduate from Carthage High School, and after that date I can begin work immediately.

I have had no practical experience in electrical work. But I have for two years made a special study of physics, in and out of school. I worked last summer in the local garage of Mr. R. S. Bryant. In addition, I have become familiar with tools in my workshop at home, so that I both know and like machinery.

For statements as to my character and ability, I refer you to R. S. Bryant, Manager Bryant's Garage; Mr. Frank Darrow (lawyer), 602 Ninth Street; W. C. Barnes, Superintendent of Schools; and C. W. Oldham, Principal of the High School—all of this city.

>Respectfully yours,
>Howard Rolfe

87. **Formal notes and replies are written in the third person** (avoiding *I, my, me, you, your*) **and permit no abbreviations except** *Mr., Mrs., Dr.*

>Mrs. Clarence King requests the company of
>Mr. Charles Eliot at dinner on Friday,
>April the twenty-fourth, at six o'clock.
>
>102 Pearl Street,
> April the seventeenth.

In accepting an invitation, the writer should repeat the day and hour mentioned, in order to avoid a misunderstanding; in declining an invitation, only the day need be mentioned. The verb used in the reply should be in the present tense; not "will be pleased to accept", or "regrets that he will be unable to accept"; but "is pleased to accept", or "regrets that circumstances prevent his accepting".

> Mr. Charles Eliot gladly accepts the
> invitation of Mrs. King to dinner on
> Friday, April the twenty-fourth, at
> six o'clock.
>
> 514 Poplar Avenue,
>   April the eighteenth.

Paragraphs

88a. The first lines of paragraphs are uniformly indented, in manuscript, about an inch; in print, somewhat less. After a sentence, the remainder of a line should not be left blank, except at the end of a paragraph.

b. The length of a paragraph is ordinarily from fifty to three hundred words, depending on the importance or complexity of the thought. In exposition, the paragraphs should be long enough to develop every idea thoroughly. Scrappy expository paragraphs arouse the suspicion that the writer is incoherent, or that he has not given sufficient thought to the subject. Short paragraphs are permissible, and even desirable, in the following cases:

PARAGRAPHS

1. In a formal introduction to the main body of a discourse, or in the formal conclusion. (In some instances the paragraph may consist of a single sentence).
2. In the body of a composition, when a brief logical transition between two longer paragraphs is necessary.
3. In short compositions on complex subjects, where space forbids the development of each thought on a proper scale. (But, as a rule, the student should limit his subject to a few simple ideas, each of which can be developed fully.)
4. In newspapers, where brevity and emphasis are required. (But the student should not take the journalistic style as a model).
5. In description or narration meant to be vivid, vigorous, or rapid.
6. In dialogue.

In representing dialogue, each speech, no matter how short, is placed in a separate paragraph.

Right:

"Listen!" he said. "There was a noise outside. Didn't you hear it?"

"No," I whispered. It was dark in the room, except for a faint light at the window, and I felt my way cautiously to his side. "What is it? Burglars?"

"I believe it is."

"I can't hear anything."

"Listen! There it is again."

"Pshaw!" I had to laugh aloud. "Thompson's cow has got into the garden again."

PARAGRAPHS

Note that a slight amount of descriptive matter may be included in a paragraph with the direct discourse, the only requirement being that a change of speaker shall be indicated by a new paragraph.

When special emphasis is desired, a quotation may be detached from a preceding introductory statement.

> Right: The speaker turned gravely about, and facing the front row, he said slowly and solemnly:
> "Small boys should be seen and not heard."

In exceptional cases a long, rapid-fire dialogue may, for purposes of compression, be placed in one paragraph. Dashes should then be used before successive quotations to indicate a change of speaker.

Omissions from a dialogue (as when only one side of a telephone conversation is reported), long pauses, and the unfinished part of interrupted statements, may be represented by a short row of dots.

Exercise:

> Arrange in paragraphs, and insert quotation marks:
> The gentleman, said the chairman, is out of order. Will the chairman, inquired Leacock, kindly explain why I am out of order? Mr. Hayman has the floor. Mr. Chairman, I had concluded my remarks, said Hayman. In that case the gentleman is in order, and the chair begs his pardon.

MISCELLANEOUS EXERCISE

The following sentences illustrate errors in the use of capitals, italics, numbers, abbreviations, etc. Make necessary changes.

1. Robert fulton's steamboat, the clermont, made its trip on the hudson in eighteen hundred and seven.
2. With 3 friends I took an automobile ride from portland over the beautiful columbia highway.
3. On our way to los angeles we left the main line of the santa fé railroad for a side trip to the grand canyon of the colorado.
4. Miss Newberry comes down the street every p. m. with a book & a music roll in her hand.
5. The no. of $ he owed us was about three thousand.
6. Thanks for your order of Mch. 5 and have given it prompt attention.
7. Rec'd yrs & beg to advise your subscription has been entered for the balance of the year.
8. The city's expenditure for st. improvement last yr. was twenty-seven thousand, two hundred and thirty-nine $ and eighteen cts.
9. The equable temperature of hawaii seemed the more remarkable to Throckmorton for his having lived in O. and Ia.
10. Please find enclosed $0.30 in stamps, for which send me delineator pattern no. four thousand, six hundred, and thirty-eight.
11. The teacher rang the bell, and 8 forlorn looking children straggled into the room.
12. Dear Jack: Yours of the 16th received. How I did enjoy hearing from you, old chap! Can't answer now. Look out for real letter about the 1st of next month. Yours truly, Chas.

MISCELLANEOUS EXERCISE

13. Trusting our acquaintance will be mutually pleasant & profitable, & assure you we are,

    Yours truly,

    Hogsett and Co.

14. Appreciate your inquiry, & in reply would say Silver Steel is made to our private formula. Agreeable to our promise, if it fails to give satisfaction, you may return it and may get your money.

15. In receipt of yours of late date, beg to state are sorry to hear of damage to mdse. in shipment. If you will send us release of bill of lading with notation of damage made by freight agent, will replace goods & trust this will be a satisfactory settlement.

PUNCTUATION

Punctuation is not used for its own sake. It is used in writing as gestures, pauses, and changes of voice are used in speaking—to add force or to reveal the precise relationship of thoughts. The tendency at present is against the lavish use of punctuation. This does not mean, however, that one may do as he pleases. In minor details of punctuation there is room for individual preference, but in essential principles all trustworthy writers agree.

The Period

90a. Place a period after a complete declarative or imperative sentence.

b. Do not separate part of a sentence from the rest of the sentence by means of a period. (See 1.)

Wrong: He denied the accusation. As every one expected him to do.
Right: He denied the accusation, as every one expected him to do.
Wrong: Anderson wrote good editorials. The best that appeared in any paper in the city.
Right: Anderson wrote good editorials, the best that appeared in any paper in the city. [Or] Anderson wrote good editorials—the best that appeared in any paper in the city.

Exception.—Condensed or elliptical phrases established by long and frequent use may be written as separate sentences. They should be followed by appropriate punctuation—usually by a period.

Examples: Yes. Of course. Really? By all means!

PUNCTUATION—THE PERIOD

Note.—The student should distinguish clearly between a subordinate clause and a main clause. A subordinate clause is introduced by a subordinate conjunction (*when, while, if, as, since, although, that, lest, because, in order that,* etc.), or by a relative pronoun (*who, which, that,* etc.). Since a subordinate clause does not express a complete thought, it cannot stand alone, but must be joined to a main clause to form a sentence.

C. Place a period after an abbreviation.

Bros. Mr. e.g. Ph.D. LL.D. etc.

If an abbreviation falls at the end of a sentence, one period may serve two functions.

Exercise:

1. The Rev Dr Martin stood in the street and read the newly painted sign: "Edgar Milton, M D"
2. A rather portly woman entered and took a seat. Making the car seem smaller than before.
3. When Hoyt left his hostess. He felt like a rudderless boat. Adrift in an uncharted sea.
4. The caps are small and can be put in the pocket during class. Which is much easier than holding a large hat.
5. Although the man also can ride on the sledge. No good driver likes to burden his huskies with the extra weight. Unless it is absolutely necessary.

The Comma

There are five principal uses of the comma:

  to separate clauses (a — d)
  to set off a parenthetical element (e)
  to mark a series (f — g)

PUNCTUATION—THE COMMA

to introduce a quotation (h)
to compel a pause for the sake of clearness (i)

91a. A comma is used between clauses joined by *but, for, and,* or any other coördinating conjunction.

Right: The hour arrived, but Forbes did not appear. [The comma emphasizes the contrast.]
Right: She was glad she had looked, for a man was approaching the house. [The comma prevents the combination *looked for a man.*]
Right: He gave the money to Burke, and Reynolds received nothing. [The comma prevents confusion.]

Exception.—If the clauses are short and closely linked in thought, the comma may be omitted (She came and she was gone in a moment. McCoy talked and the rest of us listened). If the clauses are long and complicated, a semicolon may be used (See 92b).

Note.—No comma should follow the conjunction.

Wrong: He was enthusiastic but, inexperienced.
Wrong: They went before the committee but, not one of them would answer a question.

b. Do *not* use a comma between independent clauses which are *not* joined by a conjunction. Use a period or a semicolon. (This error, the "comma splice," betrays ignorance of what constitutes a unified sentence. See 18.)

Wrong: The circus had just come to town, every one wanted to see it.
Right: The circus had just come to town. Every one wanted to see it.

PUNCTUATION—THE COMMA

Wrong: The story deals with the life of a youth, Don Juan, his mother desired to make an angel of him.
Right: The story deals with the life of a youth, Don Juan. His mother desired to make an angel of him.
Wrong: My courses required very hard study, did yours?
Right: My courses required very hard study. Did yours?
 [Or] My courses required very hard study; did yours?
Wrong: He will assist you without the slightest hesitation, indeed he will do so with alacrity.
Right: He will assist you without the slightest hesitation. Indeed he will do so with alacrity. [Or] He will assist you without the slightest hesitation; indeed he will do so with alacrity.

Exception.—Short coördinate clauses which are not joined by conjunctions, but which are parallel in structure and leave a unified impression, may be joined by commas.

Right: He sowed, he reaped, he repented.

C. An adverbial clause which precedes a main clause is usually set off by a comma.

When long:

Right: While I have much confidence in his sincerity, I cannot approve his decision. [The comma marks the meeting point of clauses too long to be easily read together. Brief clauses do not require the comma. Right: Where thou goest I will go.]

When ending in words that link themselves with words in the main clause:

Right: If Jacob finds time to plow, the garden can be planted to-morrow. [The comma prevents *plow the garden* from being read as verb and object.]

PUNCTUATION—THE COMMA

When not closely connected with the main clause in meaning:

Right: Although they were few, they were resolute. [Here the comma reveals the distinctness of the two stages of thought. In the sentence *If it freezes the skating will be good* the distinctness of the two thoughts is less emphatic, and the comma may be omitted.]

Note.—The comma is usually omitted when the adverbial clause follows the main clause.

Right: The score stood twelve to twelve when the first half ended. [The adverbial clause is linked closely with the element it modifies, the predicate; punctuation is unnecessary. If the *when* clause were placed before the element it does not modify, the subject, a comma should be inserted.]

d. Restrictive clauses should not be set off by commas; non-restrictive clauses should be set off by commas

(A restrictive clause is one inseparably connected with the noun or pronoun it modifies; to omit it would change the thought of the main clause. A non-restrictive clause is less vitally connected with the noun or pronoun; to omit it would not affect the thought of the main clause.)

Right: Men who are industrious will succeed. [The relative clause restricts the meaning; it is inseparably connected with the noun it modifies, and to omit it would change the thought of the main clause.]

Right: Thomas Carlyle, who wrote forty volumes, was of peasant origin. [The relative clause is non-restrictive; it is not inseparably connected with the noun it modifies, and to omit it would not change the thought of the main clause. Thus: Thomas Carlyle was of peasant origin.]

Right: Where is the house that Jack built? [Restrictive.]

PUNCTUATION—THE COMMA

Right: I went to Jack's house, which is across the street. [Non-restrictive.]

Wrong: Students, who are lazy, do not deserve to pass. [The sentence as it stands says that all students are lazy, and that none of them deserve to pass. Without the commas, the sentence would mean that such students as are lazy do not deserve to pass.]

Right: Students who are lazy do not deserve to pass.

The rule stated above for clauses applies also to phrases.

Right: She, hearing the voice, turned quickly. [*Hearing the voice* is non-restrictive. It does not identify *she*, and the thought of the main clause is complete without it.]

Right: Books pertaining to aeronautics are in demand. [*Pertaining to aeronautics* is restrictive. It explains what books are referred to, and without it the meaning of the main thought is changed.]

Right: Our country, made up as it is of democratic people, lacks the centralized power of a monarchy. [Non-restrictive.]

Right: A country made up of democratic people must be lacking in centralized power. [Restrictive. *Made up of democratic people* explains *country* and is essential to the thought of the sentence.]

e. Slightly parenthetical elements are set off by commas:

Direct address or explanation:

Write soon, Henry, and tell all the news.
They intend, as you know, to build a dam across the river.
His father, they say, was frugal and industrious.
I, on my part, however, am unalterably opposed to the expenditure.
First, they rented a banquet hall. In the next place, they arranged to purchase provisions.

PUNCTUATION—THE COMMA

Mild interjections:

> Well, we shall see.
> Come now, let's talk it over.
> But alas, the cupboard was bare.
> The custom is, oh, very old.

Absolute phrases:

> This being admitted, I shall proceed to my other evidence.

Geographical names which explain other names, and dates which explain other dates:

> The convention met at Madison, Wisconsin, on March 24, 1916.

Words in apposition:

> We arrived at Austin, the capital of Texas.
> It was Archie, my best friend in boyhood.

Exception.—The comma is omitted (1) When the appositive is part of a proper name. Right: William the Silent, Alexander the Great. (2) When there is unusually close connection between the appositive and the noun it modifies. Right: My one confidant was my brother Robert. (3) When the appositive is a word or phrase to which attention is called by italics or some other device which sets it apart. Right: The word *sequent* is derived from Latin. Right: The expression "That's fine" is one which I use indiscriminately.

Note.—When the parenthetical element occurs in the middle of a sentence, "set off by commas" means *punctuate before and after*.

> Wrong: I was, madam at home yesterday.
> Right: I was, madam, at home yesterday.
> Wrong: I am to say the least, provoked.
> Right: I am, to say the least, provoked.

209

PUNCTUATION—THE COMMA

f. Consecutive adjectives that modify the same noun are separated from each other by commas. If, however, the last adjective is closely linked in meaning with the noun, no comma is used before it.

Right: A short, slight, pitiable figure.
Right: A shrewd professional man. [*Shrewd* modifies, not *man* alone, but *professional man*.]
Right: A bedraggled old rooster. [*Old rooster* has almost the force of a compound word. *Bedraggled* modifies the general idea *old rooster*.]

Note.—The commas in a series of adjectives are used to separate the adjectives from each other. No comma should intervene between the final adjective and the noun. Wrong: He was only a frail, unarmed, frightened, youngster. Right: He was only a frail, unarmed, frightened youngster.

g. Words or phrases in series are separated by commas. When the series takes the form *a, b, and c,* a comma precedes the *and*.

Confusing: The railroads in question are the New York Central, Pennsylvania and Chesapeake and Ohio. [The reader might surmise that the words *Pennsylvania and Chesapeake and Ohio* represent a single line or even three different lines.]
Right: The railroads in question are the New York Central, Pennsylvania, and Chesapeake and Ohio.
Confusing: For breakfast we had oatmeal, bacon, eggs and honey. [Omission of the comma after *eggs* suggests a mixture.]
Right: For breakfast we had oatmeal, bacon, eggs, and honey.

h. A comma should follow an expression like *he said* which introduces a short quotation. (For longer or more formal quotations, use a colon.)

PUNCTUATION—THE COMMA

Right: He shouted, "Come on! I dare you!"
Right: Our captain replied, "We're ready."

But for indirect quotations, a caution is necessary. Do not place a comma between a verb and a *that* or *how* clause which the verb introduces.

Wrong: He explained, how the accident occurred.
Right: He explained how the accident occurred.
Wrong: The chauffeur told us, that the gasoline tank was empty.
Right: The chauffeur told us that the gasoline tank was empty.

i. A comma is used to separate parts of a sentence which might erroneously be read together.

Confusing: Long before she had received a letter.
Better: Long before, she had received a letter.
Confusing: We turned the corner and the horse stopped throwing us off.
Better: We turned the corner and the horse stopped, throwing us off.
Confusing: Through the alumni gathered there went a thrill of dismay.
Better: Through the alumni gathered there, went a thrill of dismay.
Wrong: For a dime you can buy two pieces of pie or cake and ice cream.
Right: For a dime you can buy two pieces of pie, or cake and ice cream.
Right: The man whom everybody had for years regarded as a crank and a weakling, is now praised for his sagacity and his strength.
Right: In a situation so critical as to require the utmost coolness of mind, he lost his wits completely. [Here the confusion might not be serious if the comma were omitted, but separation of the long introduction from the main clause is desirable.]

PUNCTUATION—THE COMMA

j. Do not use superfluous commas:

1. To mark a trivial pause:

> Needless use of comma: In the road, stood a wagon.
> Needless use of commas: The taking of notes, is a guarantee, against inattention, in class.

Slight pauses in a sentence are taken care of by the good sense of the reader. Do not sprinkle commas when the sentence is moving along freely with no complication in the thought.

> Right: In the road stood a wagon.
> Right: The taking of notes is a guarantee against inattention in class.

2. To separate an adjective from its noun:

> Wrong: A tall, solemn, antique, clock stood in the hallway. [The first two commas separate the adjectives from each other. There is no reason why *antique* should be separated from the noun.]
> Right: A tall, solemn, antique clock stood in the hallway.

3. Before the first word or phrase in a series unless the comma would be employed if the word or phrase stood alone:

> Wrong: He made a study of, gymnastics, medicine, and surgery.
> Right: He made a study of gymnastics, medicine, and surgery.
> Wrong: He had learned, to be prompt, to think clearly, and to write correctly.
> Right: He had learned to be prompt, to think clearly, and to write correctly.

PUNCTUATION—THE SEMICOLON

Exercise:

1. If you take your ax and cut a hole through the thick ice the fish will crowd about it in great numbers for air and you can spear them at will.
2. Little is known of the cliff-dwellers since they left no literature.
3. They filled the vacancies in the jury with a donkey a cat and a dog.
4. Joseph became a favored servant in the king's palace but one day he was falsely accused of a crime.
5. I blushed for ten minutes had scarcely passed since I had told him the opposite of what I was now saying.
6. I saw the girl's mother her father and her grandmother and as I surmised before she belongs to a friendly intelligent admirable old family.
7. Apparently the chap who took my umbrella isn't going to bring it back. But you know Chris I can always borrow. Stark who spent two years in Honolulu tells me I can have his umbrella because as he says he is used to rain.
8. In the midst of our preparations uncles aunts and cousins drove up. Such hilarity such merriment in welcoming them you never saw.

The Semicolon

The semicolon represents a division in thought somewhat greater than that represented by a comma, and somewhat smaller than that represented by a period. It may represent grammatical separation and logical connection at the same time; that is, it may indicate that two statements are separate units in grammar, and are yet to be taken together to form a larger unit of logic or thought.

PUNCTUATION—THE SEMICOLON

92a. **The semicolon is used between coördinate clauses which are not joined by a conjunction.** (For a possible exception see 91b.)

> Wrong: He was alarmed in fact he was terrified.
> Right: He was alarmed; in fact he was terrified.
> Right: He drew up at the curb; he leaped from the car.

Note.—Very often the writer may choose freely between the semicolon and the period; in such instances the use of the semicolon implies greater logical unity between the clauses than the use of the period would show. Unless this logical unity is distinct, the period is to be preferred.

b. **The semicolon is sometimes used between coördinate clauses which are joined by a conjunction if the clauses are long, or if the clauses have commas within themselves, or if obscurity would result were the semicolon not used.** (Otherwise, see 91a.)

> Right: Very slowly the glow in the heavens deepened and extended itself along the eastern horizon; but at last the bright-red rim of the sun showed above the crest of the hill.
> Right: He arrived, so they tell me, after nightfall; and immediately going to a hotel, called for a room.
> Confusing: She enjoyed the dinners, and the dancing, and the music, and the whole gay round of fashionable life was a delight to her.
> Better: She enjoyed the dinners, and the dancing, and the music; and the whole gay round of fashionable life was a delight to her.

c. **The semicolon is used between coördinate clauses which are joined by a formal conjunctive adverb**

PUNCTUATION—THE SEMICOLON

(*hence, thus, then, therefore, accordingly, consequently, besides, still, nevertheless,* or the like).

Wrong: We have failed in this therefore let us try something else.

Right: We have failed in this; therefore let us try something else.

Wrong: He was tattered and muddy, besides he ate like a cormorant.

Right: He was tattered and muddy; besides he ate like a cormorant.

Note 1.—If a simple conjunction like *and* is used in the sentences above, a comma will suffice. But a comma is not sufficient before a conjunctive adverb like *therefore*. Conjunctive adverbs may be clearly distinguished from simple conjunctions (See 91a). They cannot always be easily distinguished from subordinating conjunctions (see 90b, Note), but the distinction, when it can be made with certainty, is an aid to clear thinking.

Note 2.—Good usage sometimes permits a comma to be used before a conjunctive adverb in short sentences where the break in the thought is not formal or emphatic. For instance, when the conjunctive adverb *so* is used as a formal or emphatic connective, a semicolon is desirable (I won't go; so that's settled). But in the sentence, "I was excited, so I missed the target", a comma is sufficient. For the use of *so* is here informal, and probably expresses degree as well as result. (Compare "I was so excited that I missed the target").

d. The semicolon is not used before quotations, or after the "Dear Sir" in letters. Use a comma or a colon. (See 91h, 93a, and 87b.)

PUNCTUATION—THE COLON

Wrong: Mother said; "Let me get my needle."
Right: Mother said, "Let me get my needle."

Exercise:

1. The postman then approached he would surely stop I thought.
2. Fruit raised in a high altitude is likely to have excellent flavor fruit raised in a low altitude is more insipid.
3. He had a diver's apparatus therefore he thought he could easily descend to the wreck.
4. He replied "Mr. Hume I did not expect these facts to be called for hence I did not bring the exact figures."
5. He goes often to the club to the theater to the dance halls to the cabarets and to these sources one can trace his slackening of interest in the work.
6. His presence is urgently needed at the conference his influence there will be of the greatest value.
7. All went smoothly while Brutus talked then the same plebeians who showed friendly feeling toward Brutus were ready to swear allegiance to Antony.
8. I was shocked at the cold unfeeling way in which she spoke of poverty of unemployment of the condition of working men yet such was her charm I found myself nodding in agreement.

The Colon

93a. The colon is used to introduce formally a word, a list, a statement or question, a series of statements or questions, or a long quotation.

Right: Only one man stood between Burr and the presidency: Jefferson.

Right: My favorite novels are the following: *Ivanhoe, Henry Esmond,* and *The Mill on the Floss.*

Right: The difficulty is this: Where is the money to come from?

PUNCTUATION—THE COLON

Right: The measure must be considered from several standpoints: Is it timely? Is it expedient? Is it just? Is it superior to the other measures proposed?

Right: I shall do three things next year: study hard, take care of my health, and enter into various student activities.

Right: Webster concluded with the following peroration: "When my eyes turn to behold for the last time the sun in heaven," etc., etc.

b. The colon may be used before concrete illustrations of a general statement.

Right: The colors were various: blue, purple, emerald, and orange.

Right: The day was propitious: the sun shone, the birds sang, the flowers sent forth their fragrance.

Exercise:

1. There is an old proverb which argues thus You take care of the pennies and the dollars will take care of you.
2. We carry in stock sun-fast window drapery in the following colors pink pearl tan rose brown.
3. Two conditions favored an attack by our army our morale was excellent while that of the enemy was low our artillery was placed whereas that of the enemy was being shifted.
4. The chairman then submitted the recommendation of the committee The paving project should be instantly abandoned those responsible for it should be prosecuted and steps should be taken to protect the interests of the citizens.
5. Mr President I rise to answer a toast whose theme is that of the old ballad

>   Sing a song of the sea my lads
>   Yeo heave ho around
>   The anchor's up the helm's a-lee
>   Ho for the homeward bound.

217

PUNCTUATION—THE DASH

The Dash

94a. The dash may be used instead of the marks of parenthesis, especially where informality is desired.

> Right: She fell asleep—would you believe it?—in the middle of the lecture.
>
> Right: That fellow actually—of course this is between you and me—stole money from his father.

b. Insert a dash when a sentence is broken off abruptly.

> Right: The next morning—let's see, what happened the next morning?

c. The dash may be used near the end of a sentence, before a summarizing statement or an afterthought.

> Right: When you have carried in the wood and the water, and milked the cows, and fed all the stock and the poultry, and mended the harness—when you have done these things, you may consider the rest of the evening your own.
>
> Right: Barnes played a mischievous trick one day—in fact, Barnes was always into mischief.

d. The use of the dash to end sentences is childish.

> Childish: At dawn I went on deck—far off to the left was a cloud, I thought, on the edge of the water—it grew more distinct as we angled toward it—it was land—before noon we had sailed into harbor.
>
> Right: At dawn I went on deck. Far off to the left was a cloud, I thought, on the edge of the water. It grew more distinct as we angled toward it. It was land. Before noon we had sailed into harbor.

e. A dash should be made about three times as long as a hyphen; otherwise it may be mistaken as the sign of a compound word.

PUNCTUATION—PARENTHESES AND BRACKETS

Exercise:
1. Lucky persons no member of that clan is speaking find pearls in oysters.
2. Here are four tickets for the opera which I where did I put those tickets?
3. Testing the seed grain does not every up-to-date farmer know this means a better stand and a better crop.
4. If there be one state in the union Mr. President and I say it not in a boastful spirit that may challenge comparison with any other for a uniform zealous ardent uncalculating devotion to the union that state is South Carolina.
5. If you have bought the right kind of trap if you have baited it properly if you have set it in a good place if you have cleverly concealed the signs that it *is* a trap even if you have done all this you may not catch anything.

Parenthesis Marks and Brackets

95a. Parenthesis marks may be used to enclose matter foreign to the main thought of the sentence. (But see also 94a and 91e.)

Right: His testimony is conclusive (unless, to be sure, we find that he has perjured himself).

b. A comma or a semicolon used at the end of a parenthesis should as a rule follow the mark of parenthesis rather than precede it.

Right: If there is snow on the ground (and I am sure there will be), we shall have plenty of sleighing.

c. When confirmatory symbols or figures are enclosed within parenthesis marks, they should follow rather than precede the words they confirm.

Wrong: They earn (3) three dollars a day.
Right: They earn three (3) dollars a day. [Or] They earn three dollars ($3) a day.

PUNCTUATION—QUOTATION MARKS

d. **Do not use parenthesis marks to cancel a word or passage.** Draw a horizontal line through whatever is to be omitted.

e. **Brackets are used to insert explanatory matter in a quotation which one gives from another writer.** Explanatory matter inserted by the original writer is enclosed within parenthesis marks.

Right: "Bunyan's masterpiece (*Pilgrim's Progress*)," declared the lecturer, "is out of harmony with the spirit of the age that produced it [the age of the Restoration]." (Here the explanatory words *the age of the Restoration* are inserted by the person who is quoting the lecturer.)

Exercise:
1. Our terms possibly our representative stated them to you are sixty days credit or five per cent off for cash.
2. He pressed the button a dozen people press it every hour but there was no response.
3. [Insert *the tenth* as your explanation]: The witness said "On this day I saw the prisoner take the east-bound train."
4. [Insert *the gypsy moth* as the explanation of the person quoted]: "This insect destroys the foliage."
5. I am almost ready to sink ma'am beneath the confusion of addressing a lady in my nightcap here the lady hastily snatched off hers but I can't get it off ma'am here Mr Pickwick gave it a tremendous tug in proof of the statement.

Quotation Marks

96a. **Quotation marks should be used to enclose a direct, but not an indirect, quotation.**

Right: "I am thirsty," he said.
Wrong: He said "that he was thirsty."
Right: He said that he was thirsty.

PUNCTUATION—QUOTATION MARKS

b. A quotation of several paragraphs should have quotation marks at the beginning of each paragraph and at the end of the last paragraph.

c. In narrative each separate speech, however short, should be enclosed within quotation marks; but a single speech of several sentences should have only one set of quotation marks.

> Wrong: "Will you come? she pleaded.
> Certainly."
> Right: "Will you come?" she pleaded.
> "Certainly."
> Wrong: He replied, "It was not for my own sake that I did this." "There were others whom I had to consider." "I can mention no names."
> Right: He replied, "It was not for my own sake that I did this. There were others whom I had to consider. I can mention no names."

d. Quotation marks may be used with technical terms, with slang introduced into formal writing, or with nicknames; but not with merely elevated diction, with good English that resembles slang, with nicknames that have practically become proper names, or with fictitious names from literature.

> Permissible: The rime is called a "feminine rime". He is really "a corker". Their name for my friend was "Sissy".
> Better without the quotation marks: He was awed by "the grandeur of the mountains". "A humbug". "Fetch". "Stonewall" Jackson. He was a true "Rip Van Winkle".

e. Either quotation marks or italics may be used with words to which special attention is called. (See the examples under 91e, Exception, 3.) Quotation

PUNCTUATION—QUOTATION MARKS

marks are used with the titles of articles, of chapters in books, of individual short poems, and the like. Italics are used with the titles of books or of periodicals, with the names of ships, and with foreign words which are still felt to be emphatically foreign.

f. A quotation within a quotation should be enclosed in single quotation marks; a quotation within that, in double marks.

Right: "It required courage," the speaker said, "for a man to affirm in those days: 'I endorse every word of Patrick Henry's sentiment, "Give me liberty, or give me death!"' "

g. When a word is followed by both a quotation mark and a question mark or an exclamation point, the question mark or the exclamation point should come first if it applies to the quotation; last, if it applies to the main sentence.

Wrong: He shouted but one command, "Give them the bayonet"!
Right: He shouted but one command, "Give them the bayonet!"
Wrong: Did Savonarola say, "I recant?"
Right: Did Savonarola say, "I recant"?

Note.—Regarding the position of a comma, semicolon, or period at the end of a quotation, usage differs. Printers ordinarily place commas and periods inside the quotation marks, and semicolons outside, from considerations of spacing. But logic, not spacing, should determine the order, and all three marks should be treated alike. They should be placed within the quotation marks if they were a part of the original quotation;

PUNCTUATION—QUOTATION MARKS

otherwise outside. In quoting manuscript, the quotation marks should enclose exactly what is in the original. In quoting oral discourse, a certain liberty is necessarily allowed.

Correct: He said calmly, "It is I."
Also correct, but not commonly used: He said calmly, "It is I".
Correct, and in common use, but slightly illogical: He began, "Our Father which art in heaven." [The period should follow the quotation mark, since there is no period in the original quotation.]
Correct, and in common use, but slightly illogical: Can you tell me the difference between "apt," "likely," and "liable"; between "noted" and "notorious"?
Also correct: Can you tell me the difference between "apt", "likely", and "liable"; between "noted" and "notorious"?

1. **When a quotation is interrupted by such an expression as *he said*,**

    1. **An extra set of quotation marks is employed and the interpolated words are normally set off by commas.**

        Wrong: "I rise said he to second the motion."
        Right: "I rise", said he, "to second the motion."

    2. **A question mark or exclamation point should precede the interpolated expression if it would be used were the expression omitted.**

        Right: " 'May I go?' " complained father, "is all that boy can ask."
        Right: "Merciful heavens!" he cried, "we are lost."

    3. **The expression should be followed by a semicolon if the semicolon would follow the preceding words in case the expression were omitted.**

        Right: "I admit it", he said; "it is true."

PUNCTUATION—QUOTATION MARKS

4. Neither the expression nor the words following it should begin with a capital.

> Wrong: "We must be quiet", Said the old man, 'If we expect to catch sight of a squirrel."
> Right: "We must be quiet", said the old man, 'if we expect to catch sight of a squirrel."

i. An omission from a quotation is indicated by dots.

> Right: "When a word is followed by both a quotation mark and . . . an exclamation point, . . . the exclamation point should come . . . last, if it applies to the main sentence." [Abridged citation of g above.]

j. Do not use superfluous quotation marks:

1. Around the title at the head of a theme (unless it is a quoted title);
2. As a label for humor or irony.

> Superfluous: The "abstemious" Mr. Crew ate an enormous dinner.
> Better: The abstemious Mr. Crew ate an enormous dinner.

Exercise:

1. He said "that he would be back at dinner time."
2. Is your name William? I asked him. No; it was Willum.
3. The speaker said, I always admired the lines beginning, The age of chivalry is gone.
4. Did you register? I inquired. Of course. Then you can really vote? For the first time.
5. Look at the contradictory accounts of this young lawyer. We read in the various papers that he works hard; he is unscrupulous; no man makes more patriotic speeches; he robs widows; he gives to charity; he receives unearned fees from corporations; he is a man in whom all our citizens take pride.

PUNCTUATION—THE APOSTROPHE

The Apostrophe

7a. **In contracted words place the apostrophe where letters are omitted, and do not place it elsewhere.**

Wrong: does'nt, theyr'e, oclock.
Right: doesn't, they're, o'clock.

b. **To form the possessive of a noun, singular or plural, that does not end in s, add 's.**

Right: A hunter's gun, children's games, the cannon's mouth.

c. **To form the possessive of a noun, singular or plural, that ends in s, place an apostrophe after (not before) the s if there is no new syllable in pronunciation. If there is a new syllable in pronunciation, add 's.**

Wrong: Moses's mandates, Keat's poems, Dicken's novels, those hunter's guns.
Right: Moses' mandates, Keats's poems (or Keats' poems), Dickens' (or Dickens's) novels, those hunters' guns.

d. **Do not use an apostrophe with the possessive adjective *its, his, hers, ours, yours,* and *theirs.* But *one's, other's, either's* take the apostrophe.**

e. **Add 's to form the plural of letters of the alphabet, of words spoken of as words, and sometimes of numbers. But do not form the regular plural of a word by adding 's (See 77).**

Right: His *B's, 8's* (or *8s*), and *it's* look much alike.
Wrong: The Jones's, the Smith's, and the Brown's.
Right: The Joneses, the Smiths, and the Browns.

PUNCTUATION—QUESTION, EXCLAMATION

Exercise:

1. Theyre not happy without tea at four oclock.
2. I couldnt say it was hers. Youre sure it wasnt yours?
3. Each will have to take the others word for it.
4. Ones *Ts* may look like *7s*. At least many peoples do. Im not speaking of yours, of course. Youre a very good writer.
5. He got down his mothers copy of Burns poems, and read one of the Scotch bards lyrics, The Banks o Doon.

The Question Mark and the Exclamation Point

98a. Place a question mark after a direct question, but not after an indirect question.

> Wrong: What of it. What does it matter.
> Right: What of it? What does it matter?
> Wrong: He asked whether I belonged to the glee club?
> Right: He asked whether I belonged to the glee club.

Note.—When the main sentence which introduces an indirect question is itself interrogatory, a question mark follows.

> Right: Did she inquire whether you had met her aunt?

b. A question mark is often used within a sentence, but should not be followed by a comma, semicolon, or period.

> Wrong: "What shall I do?," he asked.
> Right: "What shall I do?" he asked.
> Wrong: But where are the stocks?, the bonds?, the evidences of prosperity?
> Right: But where are the stocks? the bonds? the evidences of prosperity?

PUNCTUATION—EXERCISE

c. A question mark within parentheses may be used to express uncertainty as to the correctness of an assertion.

Right: Shakespeare was born April 23 (?), 1564.
Right: In 1340 (?) was born Geoffrey Chaucer.

d. The use of a question mark as a label for humor or irony is childish.

Superfluous: Immediately the social lion (?) rose to his feet.
Better: Immediately the social lion rose to his feet.

e. The exclamation point is used after words, expressions, or sentences to show strong emotion.

Right: Hark! I hear horses. Give us a light there, ho!

Note.—The lavish use of the exclamation point is not in good taste. Unless the emotion to be conveyed is strong, a comma will suffice. See 91e.

Exercise:

1. "Is it you, Mr. Webster," she inquired.
2. "What have you in that basket?," asked the wolf, "and where are you going?."
3. Shall we stroll by the lake play the phonograph read What is your choice.
4. How he will succeed in later life is a question I cannot answer.
5. We have other tasks now. Farewell. Good luck.

99. EXERCISE IN PUNCTUATION

Punctuate the following sentences:

A.

1. Winters over springs here
2. I wanted to go but I couldnt

PUNCTUATION—EXERCISE

3. William the Conqueror being refused the crown had taken it by force
4. The food was simple soup fish and brown bread
5. Mrs Bushby who was sweeping had no time to talk to the agent who rang her doorbell
6. Imogens stepmother the queen appeared to be kind she was in reality deceitful and cruel
7. Their money was invested in oil stock and get rich quick concerns hence it is not surprising that they lost it all
8. The uncle had been called Napoleon the Great the nephew was now called Napoleon the Little
9. There said Mr Swiveller its twelve oclock First you eat this soup and then youll see whats next
10. A tonsure says the dictionary this is what I told you all along is a shaven head
11. Four dollars and seventy five cents cried the auctioneer and how his tongue rattled going going wholl give me five
12. He did not like Fox he did not like Reynolds he did not like Nelson Chatham Burke he was testy at the idea of all innovations and suspicious of all innovators

B.

1. Its a long winding smoke filled tunnel
2. He had a bandage round his head which was aching
3. They had potato races fat mens races and three legged races
4. When one wishes to stop the feet are simply pressed hard on both pedals
5. Dont be sorry for me indeed I am quite happy
6. It was a very dark miserable place low and damp the walls were disfigured by patches of mould
7. Truly said the speaker these three Franklin Lincoln and Mark Twain are of the soil American
8. There are three types of automobile gears the planetary the electric and the selective the last named being the most common

PUNCTUATION—EXERCISE

9. Night had fallen nevertheless Whitcomb after lighting a lantern set out on foot
10. Joes hair is wet is yours Im sure yes you boys have been swimming
11. Said Joyce If you wish Ill explain the provisions of the income tax That said Sullivan is what Ive been hoping some one would do for me the task is too hard
12. Mens hearts wait upon us mens lives hang in the balance mens hopes call upon us to say what we will do

C.

1. Its the northern lights Laura
2. Ones rubber boots come in handy for the gutters are full
3. His voice dropped an eye at the keyhole was proof that they were being spied upon
4. Oh pshaw grunted Atkins I cant make heads or tails of thermostatic lines on a weather map can you
5. Everything was locked up the coal cellar the bread box the meat safe were all padlocked
6. The sum for which Manhattan Island was bought about twenty four dollars wouldnt buy a square meal in some of the high priced cafés now
7. She did not go to Rome she went to Genoa
8. Smith has become rich consequently he and his family must shut themselves off from the world by a high fence
9. Ill tell you lets ask Celia Shes a wise one shell know
10. The island of Malta which we now sighted may have been the island which was the home of Prospero and Miranda
11. Some stars it has been determined are many times larger than the sun and their distance from us past all possibility of doubting is far greater than the distance of the sun from the earth
12. Lafayette was intrusted by Washington with all kinds of service the laborious and complicated which required skill and patience the perilous that demanded nerve and we see him performing all with entire success

PUNCTUATION—EXERCISE

D.

1. He patted me on the head and the horse started
2. Whenever any one knocked the dog leaped up and barked
3. It was the first half warm hesitating undecided day of spring
4. This is he the shepherd boy who had no counselor but the voices of winds and streams
5. Home husband children all these she had lost in the war
6. Islands lying on all sides of us made the route to Alaska one of constant wild and extraordinary beauty
7. The noise was well did you ever hear a buzz saw cutting through a knot it was something like that only worse
8. You try to read but the book is uninteresting hence you throw it across the table
9. In glades where only deer should run armies are standing in wide fields the harvests are trodden under the feet of cavalry
10. He lamented not without pathos in his after life that his education had been neglected
11. Now said Dick walking up and down Id give a small fortune if I had it to know what she thinks of me
12. We shall deal with our economic system as it is and as it may be modified not as it might be if we had a clean sheet of paper to write upon and step by step we shall make it what it should be in the spirit of those who question their own wisdom and seek counsel and knowledge not shallow self satisfaction or the excitement of excursions whither they cannot tell

E.

1. Trucks drove up the Hickses were moving
2. Aunt Hilda has I should think about three bushels of apples drying on the roof
3. Thats not all theres another armful in the garden
4. They stole the savings of poor people they are wolves in sheeps clothing

PUNCTUATION—EXERCISE

5. The human frame may be considered as an instrument of warning the stomach that dinner time has come the joints that bad weather may be expected
6. Ones home was in Butte Montana but we could not raise the money for so long a trip a hundred dollars
7. We painters he said call these colors warm red yellow and orange And are not green blue and violet I asked the colors you call cool
8. The end of the story contained a surprise therefore we were all pleased
9. This man Abelard was probably the most magnetic teacher the lecturer declared who ever lived he could retreat to the country and in a short time be surrounded by thousands of students
10. He did his best according to his light what virtue he knew he tried to practice what knowledge he could master he strove to acquire
11. Our duty is to cleanse to reconsider to restore to correct the evil without impairing the good to purify and humanize every process of our common life without weakening or sentimentalizing it
12. He is at rest now the stalwart brave old champion whose face and bearing were so austere and whose heart was so full of tenderness who began his career with a pathetic plea for universal peace and charity and whose life was an arduous incessant never resting struggle which left him all covered with scars

F.

1. There lay some artichokes eating apples too
2. If you rob the beehive in late autumn leave some honey for the bees else they will starve
3. The horse held his head high and placed his ears well back he had an I dare you look in his eyes
4. Wash the rags until they are clean then put them in the sun to dry

PUNCTUATION—EXERCISE

5. The kite that boy was always flying kites was tangled in the telephone wires
6. The old sheik climbed upon the camel for miles he had walked through hot desert sand
7. The method is this by soaking the garment in hot salt water you set the color by ironing it you shrink the cloth
8. Isnt that the Chamber of Commerce Tom Gwendolin asked
9. The pistons crank shaft gears and transmission are the vital parts of an automobile that is why they run in oil
10. Oh its Mr James she exclaimed Glad to see you when did you get back
11. The king is said not to have cared for Shakespeare or tragedy much farces and pantomimes were his joy and especially when a clown swallowed a carrot or a string of sausages he would laugh so outrageously that the lovely princess by his side would have to say My gracious monarch do compose yourself
12. All the world knows the story of his malady all history presents no sadder figure than that of the old man blind and deprived of reason wandering through the rooms of his palace addressing imaginary parliaments reviewing fancied troops and holding ghostly courts

G.

1. No gentlemen believe me your course is wrong you are sowing the whirlwind
2. He had a business like step and an Im ready lets go expression on his face
3. They had the simplest pleasures the very mildest and simplest pleasures little country dances or playing on the piano or reading the *Spectator*
4. Garments made of wool may be protected by moth balls you know napthaline they tell me will protect your furs
5. Mrs Westlake wheels an old baby buggy to the market and into it she puts all her purchases cabbage apples bacon and cottage cheese

PUNCTUATION—EXERCISE

6. Well listen then will you he demanded and trembling he added you must help me for two reasons first my money is gone and second my people are sick.
7. He looked proudly at the only property he owned in the world an old coat a rusty gun and a hungry horse
8. This is what he saw in the tent amidst great shadows a candle flared on the table was spread an enormous map over the table bent a man sticking pins in the map measuring plucking out the pins and thrusting them in again
9. She never went out or had a clean face or took off the coarse apron or looked out of the window or stood at the street door for a breath of air or had any rest whatever
10. Now for a yellow pup one fishs tail is not enough so on he went until he came into a yard where lay a wealth of bones big bones little bones juicy bones old bones and every kind of bone dear to dog hearts
11. Lamb wrote for the most part of familiar city life of streets crowds churches concerts and picture galleries Stevenson wrote best of the wide out of doors the sea the mountains or lonely rambles in strange corners of the world
12. He spoke and in the measured cadences of his quiet voice there was intense feeling but no declamation no passionate appeal no superficial or feigned emotion it was simply colloquy a gentleman conversing

100. GENERAL EXERCISE

Improve the following sentences, making as many changes as are necessary to express the thought clearly and accurately.

A.

1. He pretends like he don't know.
2. No one likes you to be preaching at them.
3. George brings in the mail and places them on the table.
4. Clothes with a nap, you can hardly brush the lint off them.
5. He spoke a strange jargon, which nobody could tell what it meant.
6. She said, "Yes; it is me." Whom do you suppose it was?
7. He assured me the garment was all wool. Which contained no wool at all.
8. The rules of football have changed more in the past fifteen years than any other sport.
9. Rec'd your welcome letter last night, you cannot imagine how glad I was to receive it.
10. A great deal of the grains would not be shattered if the harvesting was cut before the wheat was so ripe.
11. Only at two hours of the day did he ever feel lonely,—in the bleakness of dawn, when the long evenings seemed endless.
12. Coming back from Africa with a load of slaves, a fire broke out, followed by a high wind and a rough sea.
13. Mahomet grew to be a slender, bright-eyed boy, who helped his grandfather with the sheep and other duties, and a clear thinker.
14. When he finally reached camp through the aid of a guide he looks more like a tramp than anything I can think of, being very disreputable looking.
15. I expect my college education to broaden my views upon political and economic happenings, and deciding these

GENERAL EXERCISE

questions intelligently, learn human nature and act accordingly, to know and like books, and equip me to earn a good, honest living in the world.

B.

1. A young lady and myself went walking.
2. Chewing gum eats up more money than public schools.
3. Carlyle if living today I think he would like Vachel Lindsay.
4. After walking for half an hour, the stream turned sharply to the left.
5. The eagle has a hooked beak and builds his nest in inaccessible places.
6. He ordered bread with his roast beef and gravy which cost him only five cents.
7. Father explained that bees have only one queen, which are in that respect unlike other insects.
8. Paul of Thebes lived in the desert on dates and water to eat, and using palm leaves for clothing.
9. A base on balls is when the pitcher has four times failed to throw the ball across the plate, not too low or high.
10. He showed us how to make a whistle out of a hickory twig. Also little crowns and baskets what he cut out of oak acorns.
11. They say that at one o'clock being still digesting dinner facts are not impressed very vividly upon your mind so are apt to leave you.
12. His faults are high temper, he is careless, and a tendency to want more than his share of things.
13. My advice is this: to give an honest measure of work to your employer, that you should not engage in social diversion very often, and seizing every opportunity to hear good music.
14. One man reads the copy aloud and the other scans the proof and the second man at least must be an expert, and he gets better pay but even his pay is not liberal.

GENERAL EXERCISE

15. You plant a few sweet potatoes in a hotbed and the slips come up very thick and you pull them off and transplant them in the garden, making a hole in the well-pulverized ground into which you place the slip, and filling the hole with water before you pack the earth around the plant.

C.

1. Lloyd George though he had trouble in Ireland he stands very high.
2. He use to feel bad about it, but he don't no more.
3. The headlock is the most brutal of any other hold in wrestling.
4. The ground is harrowed after it is plowed. This helping to retain the moisture.
5. The long coat's bulge was caused by him wearing a sword under it.
6. I was surprised to hear that he went to the poor house because he was rich.
7. There was a high picket fence yet to be climbed, which resulted in tearing my new dress.
8. He carries a small, black medicine case in his hand, and in his body a big heart.
9. On the other side were some large two-story buildings built of stone, and had red tile roofs.
10. While typing the letter she made a carbon copy. Which carbon copy she placed in the office files.
11. The lack of lubricating oil, the car did not get the full benefit of his lavish use of gasoline.
12. No one will say that illiterate foreigners make better, or as good citizens, than those who are educated.
13. By finding such pictures and descriptions in the catalog, it does not prove that the articles themselves are superior.
14. Eat half a dozen walnuts each night before you go to bed which will be good for your health.
15. Before I went to college I remember of students who on celebrating an athletic victory acted very unnecessary

GENERAL EXERCISE

then I thought, but now I see it in a different light, and I realize I treated them very unjust.

D.

1. Marie could skip a rope long as any girl.
2. In the theater's lobby was her and her escort.
3. They expected to have seen him that evening.
4. Your dog don't seem to be very friendly to me.
5. I do not think *Dream Children* empty and vague like most people.
6. On the dresser was a photograph and some choice bits of china.
7. Men are not afraid to lose their lives that their country might be saved.
8. Lowell's choice of subjects do not cover as wide a scope as many essays.
9. You can more quickly cut through the log with a saw than an ax can.
10. Mrs. Roberts noticed the coiffeur of a girl in a pea-green dress that was passing.
11. There is some improvements which are needed in Rocky Ford, however. For instance, a park and a public playground.
12. The secretary called me on the telephone, stating that there would be a meeting that afternoon, and be sure and come.
13. Less care is necessary with an old car because they are worn and will not heat a bearing so quickly as a new one.
14. King Winter had shaken his head during the night, and out of the surrounding clouds had fallen countless white diamonds that covered the entire world with a warm blanket.
15. Washing the dishes and scrubbing the floor, the thought came that if an education was ever to be had, it must be now.

GENERAL EXERCISE

E.

1. Praise some one a little, and see how pleased they are.
2. The room was attractive, although it lacked warmth and being private.
3. The strong arm of the law has waded into the affair.
4. He cannot join us, not but what he wants to.
5. The cup and vase is of exquisite china, and very expensive.
6. Near the crib lay a piece of fly paper where the baby slept.
7. He was very tired as an outcome from the hard work he had done.
8. She is fond of the piano, which she indulges frequently to the distraction of the neighbors.
9. A second-hand car is wanted by one of our customers with six cylinders and a closed body.
10. In applying for a job there are three things which will always be in your favor if you do them.
11. Reading the two plays *As You Like It* and *King Henry the Fifth, As You Like It* was found to be the most interesting.
12. I noticed they didn't use words quite like I did; for instance, their word for new potatoes are spuds.
13. The gas rushed out through the puncture when the balloon begins to descend.
14. Being a very ordinary-looking dog, I wanted to bestow an extraordinary name. After thinking the matter over for a long time, he was named Zeroweather. He had only three good legs, caused by freezing one of them.
15. He wished to protect his family financially. Taking out life insurance is one of the best methods of affording financial protection for one's family. Some one had told him this. The result was that he began to investigate life insurance.

F.

1. The colt should be accustom to harness.
2. Billboards are a fine place to be advertised on.

GENERAL EXERCISE

3. Christmas time a happy event happened in our family.
4. Ben Davis apples are not nowhere near so good as Jonathans.
5. Making great efforts, the entire field was mowed in one day.
6. The swimmer lays on his left side and reaches forward with his right arm.
7. I could not hear the speaker only indistinctly, which had a sleepy influence on me.
8. Every Easter when a boy, my mother wore a new hat which all the other women were openly envious.
9. She said that black tea was horrible, any one in their right mind wouldn't think of drinking it.
10. The things to do in planting strawberries are: pick out site, prepare the ground, plants to be selected, and then be set out.
11. There is an association, and it is named the Automobile Association, to which prudent owners of automobiles should belong for the sake of the protection it gives them and their automobiles.
12. The diagram on which the plays were drawn was about ten by fourteen inches, I should judge, in size, from where I stood, which was laid out like a football gridiron, in red ink.
13. The lamp upon the cotter's table having burned low, the dog and cat sleeping peacefully by the open fire, while the old wife, reclining in her easy chair, knitting to the rhythmic sound of the cotter's measured breathing.
14. When I first saw the lake I knew it to be Chilly Pond, of which I had heard so much about. And soon to become a freshman, a shiver ran down my back. A fine place for a bath I thought a fine place for a bath and the ground covered with snow.
15. The main reason that all students that enter colleges and universities do not finish their work is because they had an easy course in high school and graduated without studying and when he enters college he tries bluffing his way through and finds out that he can't get through

GENERAL EXERCISE

that way and he begins to blame the instructors and thinks they are taking their spite out on him, this generally results in failure to reach the desired goal so he quits.

G.

1. He was often whipped when a child which was bad.
2. I never go to the office without I see the ragged woman with her poor baby selling papers.
3. The reason why I like Spanish best is I lived in Texas and learned to speak their language.
4. My greatest ambition was to ride my uncle's horse. I was named after him, and went to visit him often.
5. In most of these stories the beginning of the story gave me an idea of the kind of story it would be.
6. An owl car passes only every two hours during the night on this street, charging a twenty cent fare, which is inconvenient for people in this suburb.
7. By looking at a person's clothes, they can not be placed accurately in the scale of intelligence, must be an admitted fact.
8. Knowing that he is in the hands of the enemy, and in order to save himself and his own life, he revealed the secrets of his battalion.
9. The shelf held a queer-looking row of volumes. Some small, some bulky; some paper-backed, some leather-bound. Some greasy and much-handled. Some obviously unread.
10. I awoke several times to find the ship rocked, during the night, by the tremendous wind, as a babe is rocked by its mother, in my narrow berth.
11. During examination week is a certain something which permeates the atmosphere which is most depressing which prevents one from doing their best.
12. He had studied various kinds of mountain animals. For example. The beaver, the deer, the lynx, the wild sheep.

GENERAL EXERCISE

But found the courageous, unapproachable mountain sheep the most interesting of any other of them.

13. As I took quite a few "bird class hikes" last term looking for birds, I will explain why I dislike them. The first few were successful, but later on the students made so much noise they could not find them.

14. Although Lamb's life was rather sad and full of worries, both financial and because of his own ill health as well as some of the rest of his family, these qualities of his environment did not get into his writing much.

15. An interesting essay I read is called *A Dissertation on Roast Pig*. It describes the way by which man first learned to eat cooked meat. Through an accident one day a Chinaman's house was burned and a litter of pigs which were kept in the house were roasted nicely. His sons were first to discover that the pigs were good to eat. They, after the fire had subsided somewhat, got their fingers burnt by handling the roasted pigs and put them into their mouths to cool them, discovering that roast pigs was very good eating.

INDEX

The numbers refer to articles.

Abbreviations, 83, 90c
Absolute expressions
  Defined, 58
  Punctuation of, 91e
Accept and *except*, 67
Ad, 68
Addresses, 87b, 87e
Adjectives
  Classes of, 58
  Comparison of, 58
  Distinguished from adverbs, 56
  In a series, 91f, 91j2
Adverbs,
  Classes of, 58
  Comparison of, 58
  Distinguished from adjectives, 56
Affect and *effect*, 67
Aggravate, 68
Agreement
  Of pronouns, 51, 50i
  Of verbs, 52
Ain't, 68
All right, 68
Allusion and *illusion*, 67
Almost, Position of, 27
Already and *all ready*, 67
And before a subordinate phrase or clause, 16, 17
And used to excess, 14
And which construction, 17
Antecedent
  Defined, 58
  Faulty reference to, 20–23
Anybody, Number of, 51a
Apostrophe
  In contractions, 97
  With possessive, 97, 50f

Application for a position, 87g
Articles, Omission of, 3
As, Incorrect use of, 50a, 68
Aspect of the verb, 58
Auxiliary
  Defined, 58
  Use of, 55e
Awful, Abuse of, 68

Balanced sentence, 45
Balanced structure, 30, 45
Barbarisms, 66
Be, Nominative with, 50c
Because clauses, 5
Because of phrases, 5 Note
Both . . . and, 31
Brackets, 95e
Brevity for emphasis, 41, 60
Business letters, 87c
Bust or *busted*, 68
But used to excess, 38 Note.

Can and *may*, 67
Cannot help but, 34
Capitals, 81
Case
  Defined, 58
  Use of, 50
Cause, Inaccurate statement of, 5
Caused by, 5 Note, 23, 68
Change in number or person, 33
Change in subject or voice, 32
Change in tense, 33, 55
Choppy sentences, 13
Claim, 68
Clauses
  Cause, 5

INDEX

The numbers refer to articles.

Clauses—*continued*
  Coördinated loosely, 14, 12
  Defined, 58
  House-that-Jack-built, 38
  Misplaced, 24
  Misused as sentences, 1, 90b
  Restrictive and non-r., 91d
  Subordinate. Not to be used as complete sentences, 1
  Subordination faulty, 15
  To be reduced to phrases, 60
  When or *where* clauses, 6
Clearness, 20–39
Climax, 44
Coherence, 24–29
Collective nouns, Number of, 51c
Colloquialisms, 65
Colon, 93
Comma, 91, 92c Notes 1 and 2, 95b
  After quotation, 96 Note
  "Comma splice" or "comma fault," 18
  Not used after question mark, 98b
Comparison of adjectives and adverbs, 58
Comparisons, Inaccurate, 4
Compound sentence structure in excess, 12, 14
Compound words, 78
Concreteness, 63
Conjugation, 58
Conjunctions
  Defined, 58
  List of, 36
  Omitted, 37
  Repeated carelessly, 38
Conjunctive adverbs
  Defined, 58
  Punctuation with, 92c
Connectives, 8, 36, 37, 38
Consonants
  Between syllables, 71, 85
  Final (in spelling), 75

Construction
  Incomplete, 2
  Mixed, 34
  Split, 28
Contractions
  Apostrophe with, 97
  When proper, 65b
Coördination, Excessive, 12, 14
Correlatives, 31
Could of, 68

Dangling gerund, 23
Dangling participle, 23
Dash, 94
Dates, Writing of, 84, 91e
Declension, 58
Definition, 6 Note
Dialogue
  Paragraphing, 88c
  Punctuation before, 91h, 93a
  Punctuation in, 96
Diction, Faulty (list), 68
Different than, 68
Divided reference, 20
Don't, 51d
Double capacity, Words in, 57
Double negative, 34 Note
Drownded, 68
Due to, Proper use of, 5 Note, 23 Note, 68

Each, Number of, 51a
ei or *ie,* 74
Either, Number of, 51a
Either . . . or, 31
Ellipsis
  Defined, 58
  Misuse of, 3, 23 Note
Emigrate and *immigrate,* 67
Emphasis
  By brevity, 41
  By position, 40
  By repetition, 47
  By separation, 41
  By subordination, 42, 14
  By variety, 48
Enthuse, 68

INDEX

The numbers refer to articles.

Etc., Use of, 68
Euphemism, 61
Ever, Position of, 27
Every, every one, everybody, Number of, 51a
Exact connective, 36
Exact word, 62
Exclamation point, 98e

Figures, Use of, 84
Figures of speech, Mixed, 35
Final consonant (in spelling), 75
Final *e* before a suffix, 76
Fine, Abuse of, 68
Fine writing, 61
Flowery language, 61
Formal invitations, 87h
Former, 68

Gent, 68
Geographical names, 91e
Gerund
    Dangling, 23
    Defined, 58
    With possessive, 50g
Good Usage, 65, 66
Gotten, 68
Grammar, 50–59
Grammatical terms, 58
Guess, 68

Hackneyed expressions, 61
Had ought, 68
Handwriting, 80c
Hanged and *hung*, 67
Healthy and *healthful*, 67
Historical present, 33 Note
However, Position of, 27
Human, humans, 68
Hygienic and *sanitary*, 67
Hyphen
    Between syllables, 85
    In compound words, 78

Idioms, 65
Illogical thought, 4, 5, 6, 7

Imagery mixed, 35
Impersonal construction. Needless use of, 60
Improprieties, 66
Incomplete construction, 2
Indefinite *it, you, they*, 22 Note
Indention of paragraphs, 88
Independent ideas, 10
Infinitive
    Case with, 50e
    Defined, 58
    Sign of, to be repeated, 37
    Split, 28
    Tense of, 55
Inflection, 58
Instants and *instance*, 67
Interjections
    Defined, 58
    Punctuation of, 91e, 98e
Invitations, Formal, 87h
Is when clauses, 6
Is where clauses, 6
Italics, 82, 96e
Its (possessive adjective), without apostrophe, 50f, 97d

Kind of, 68

Later and *latter*, 67
Lead and *led*, 67
Learn and *teach*, 67
Leave and *let*, 67
Length of paragraph, 88b
Length of sentences, 12, 13, 48b
Less and *fewer*, 67
Letters, 87
Liable and *likely*, 67
Lie and *lay*, 59D, 67
Like (for *as*), 67, 68
List
    Of connectives, 36
    Of grammatical terms, 58
    Of principal parts, 54
    Of words confused in meaning, 67
    Of words confused in spelling, 73

INDEX

The numbers refer to articles.

List—*continued*
  For spelling, 79
  Of words incorrectly used, 68
  Of words logically akin, 72
Loan, 68
Locate, 68
Logic, 4, 5, 6, 7
Logical Agreement, 4, 5, 6
Logical Sequence, 25
Lose and *loose,* 67
Lots of, 68

Majority and *plurality,* 67
Manuscript, 80
Might of, 68
Misplaced word, 27
Mixed constructions, 34
Mixed imagery, 35
Modal aspects, 58
Mode
  Definition of, 58
  Use of subjunctive, 55d
Modifiers
  Grouping of, 24, 25
  Needless separation of, 24, 27
  Squinting, 26
  Wrongly used as sentences, 1, 90b
Money, 84c
Most (for *almost*), 66, 68
Myself, Needlessly used for *I* or *me,* 68

Negative, Double, 34 Note
Neither, Number of, 51a
Neither . . . nor, 31
Nice, Inaccurate use of, 62, 68
Nicknames, Quotations with, 96d
Not only . . . but also, 31
Nouns, Classes of, 58
Number
  Collective nouns, 51c
  Each, Every, etc., 51a
  Of verbs, 52
  Shift in, 33
  These kind, etc., 51b

Numbers, Use of, 84
  Formation of plural, 77d, 97e

O and *Oh,* 68
Objective case, 50d, 50e
Off of, 68
Omission
  Of words, 3
  From quotations, 96i
Only, Position of, 27
Outlines, 86
Overlapping thought, 8 Note
Owing to, Proper use of, 5 Note

Paragraphs, 88
Parallel structure, 30, 31, 45
Parenthesis and parenthetical elements, 91e, 94a, 95
Participle
  Dangling, 23
  Definition of, 58
Parts of speech, 58
Party, Abuse of, 68
Passive voice, not emphatic, 46
Past perfect tense, 55
Past tense, Wrong forms of, 54
Period, 90, 91b, 92a Note
  After quotation, 96g Note
  Not used after question mark, 98b
"Period blunder," 1, 90b
Periodic sentence, 43
Person, Change in, 33
Phonetic spelling, 71 Note
Phrases
  Absolute, 91e
  Defined, 58
  Not to be used as sentences, 1 Note
Plurals, Spelling of, 77
Poetry to be separated from prose, 41, 80b
Point of view, Shift in, 32
Ponderous language, 60

INDEX

The numbers refer to articles.

Possessive
  With gerund, 50g
  Apostrophe with, 50f, 97
  Inanimate objects in, 50h
Practical and *practicable*, 67
Predicate adjective, 58
Predicate noun, 58
Prefixes, 72
Prepositions
  Defined, 58
  Omitted, 3, 37
  Repeated carelessly, 38
Principal and *principle*, 67
Principal parts, 54
Pronouns
  Agreement with antecedent, 50i
  Case of, 50
  Kinds of, 58
  Reference of, 20, 21, 22
  Wrong use of *myself, yourself*, for *I, me, you*, 68
Pronunciation as a guide to spelling, 71
Proof and *evidence*, 67
Proposition, Synonyms for, 62
Proven, 68
Pseudo- and *quasi-*, 67

Question mark, 98
Quiet and *quite*, 67
Quotation marks *vs.* italics, 82a Note 2, 96e
Quotations
  Punctuation before, 91h, 92d, 93a
  Punctuation of, 96

Reason, Statement of, to be completed by a *that* clause, 5
Redundance, 60
Reference
  Ambiguous, 20
  Broad, 22
  Divided, 20
  Impersonal, 22 Note

Reference—*continued*
  Remote, 20
  To a clause, 22
  To a title, 21 Note
  To an unemphatic word, 21
  Weak, 21
Reflexive wrongly used for the simple pronoun, 68
Repetition
  Of connectives, good, 37; bad, 38
  Of structure, good, 47b; bad, 48b
  Of words, good, 47a; bad, 48a
Respectfully and *respectively*, 67
Restrictive and non-restrictive clauses, 91d
Right smart, 68
Rise and *raise*, 59D, 67

Said, Synonyms for, 62
Same, Abuse of, 68
Scrappy sentences, 13
Semicolon, 91b, 92, 95b
  After quotation, 96g Note
  Not used after question mark, 98b
Sequence of tense, 55
Sequence of thought, 25
Series, Punctuation of, 91f, 91g, 91j3
Shall and *will*, 53
Shift in number, person, or tense, 33
Shift in subject or voice, 32
Should and *would*, 53
Sit and *set*, 59D, 67
Slang, 66
  Quotations with, 96d
So, 36 Note, 68
Some, Abuse of, 68
Somewheres, 68
Sound, 64
Spacing, 80b
Specific words, 63

247

INDEX

The numbers refer to articles.

Spelling, 70–79
Split construction, 28
Split infinitive, 28
Squinting, 26
Stationary and *stationery*, 67
Statue, stature, and *statute,* 67
Stringy sentences, 12, 14
Subject in nominative case, 50a
Subjunctive mode
  Defined, 58
  Use of, 55d
Subordinating conjunctions
  Defined, 58
  Enumerated, 36
Subordination
  And which, 17
  Faulty, 15, 16, 17, 42
  Necessary, 12, 13, 14
Substantive defined, 58
Such, 68
Suffixes, 75, 76
Superlative degree in comparisons, 4, 58
Sure and *surely,* 68
Suspicion, 68
Syllabication, 85
Syntax defined, 58

Tautology, 60 Note
Technical terms, Quotations with, 96d
Tense
  In dependent clauses, 55a
  In general statements, 55c
  Past perfect, 55b
  Sequence of, 55
  Shift in, 33
Than or *as,* Case of pronouns after, 50a
That there, 68
Them (misused as adjective), 68

These kind, 51b
Those, Omission of relative clause after, 2, 68
Thought undeveloped, 7
Title
  Capitals in, 81
  Quoted (books, periodicals, etc.), 82a, 96e
  Reference to, 21 Note
  Spacing, etc., 80a, 96j
Transitions, 8, 36
Transpire, 68
Triteness, 61

Undeveloped thought, 7
Unity, 10-19
Upside-down subordination, 15
Usage, Good, 65, 66

Verb, Forms of the, 58
Verbals, 58

Ways, 68
Weak reference, 21
Where at, 68
While, Abuse of, 36
Who, whoever, 50b
Win out, 68
Woods, 68
Wordiness, 60
Words
  Confused in meaning, 67
  Confused in spelling, 73
  Double capacity of, 57
  Misused, 68
  Omission of, 3
Would of, 68

Yourself wrongly used for *you,* 68

		1	2	3
	COMPLETENESS OF THOUGHT	Fragments misused as sentences	Incomplete constructions	Necessary words omitted
	UNITY OF THOUGHT	10 Independent ideas	11 Excessive detail	12 Stringy sentences to be broken up	13 Choppy sentences to combine
	CLEARNESS OF THOUGHT	20 Divided reference	21 Weak reference	22 Broad reference	23 Dangling participle or gerund
		30 Parallel structure	31 Correlatives	32 Shift in subject or voice	33 Shift in number, person, or tense
	EMPHASIS	40 Emphasis by position	41 Emphasis by separation	42 Emphasis by subordination	43 Periodic sentence
GRAMMAR		50 Case	51 Number	52 Agreement	53 *Shall* and *will*
DICTION		60 Wordiness	61 Triteness	62 The exact word	63 Concreteness
SPELLING		70 Recording errors	71 Pronouncing accurately	72 Logical kinship	73 Superficial resemblance List
MISCELLANEOUS		80 Manuscript	81 Capitals	82 Italics	83 Abbreviation
PUNCTUATION		90 Period	91 Comma	92 Semicolon	93 Colon

(Left margin label: SENTENCE STRUCTURE)

	5	6	7	8	9
risons mplete ought	Cause and reason	*is when* or *is where* clauses	Undeveloped thought	Transitions	Exercise
4 ssive nation	15 Subordination of the main thought	16 Subordination thwarted by *and*	17 *and which* constructions	18 The comma	19 Exercise
4 eral erence	25 Logical sequence	26 Squinting modifier	27 Misplaced word	28 construction	29 Exercise
4 xed uctions	35 Mixed imagery	36 The exact connective	37 Connective to be repeated	38 Connective not to be repeated	39 Exercise
4 er of max	45 Balanced sentence	46 The weak passive voice	47 Repetition effective	48 Repetition offensive	49 Exercise
54 cipal rts	55 Tense mode auxiliary	56 Adjective and adverb	57 Word in a double capacity	58 List of the terms of grammar	59 Exercise
64 und	65 Idioms Colloquialisms	66 Barbarisms Slang	67 Words confused in meaning	68 Glossary of faulty diction	69 Exercise
74 nd *ie*	75 Doubling a final consonant	76 Dropping final *e*	77 Plurals	78 Compounds	79 Spelling list
84 bers	85 Syllabication	86 Outlines	87 Letters	88 Paragraphs	89 Exercise
94 ash	95 Parenthesis Brackets	96 Quotation marks	97 Apostrophe	98 Question and exclamation marks	99 Exercise